Bill & Flo

LISTENING
TO THE GRASS GROW

LISTENING TO THE GRASS GROW

by
Harry C. 'Cuz' Bagley
illustrated by
Thomas Bevel

ISBN 0-9619190-0-0

Listening to the Grass Grow
Copyright ©1987
Richard H. Bagley
in Association with
The Cherokee Scout
All rights reserved
Printed in the United States of America

This book is produced on acid-free paper
that exceeds the minimum standards set by the
National Historical Publications and Records Commission.

Library of Congress Cataloging-in-Publication Data

   Bagley, Harry C. (Harry Cecil), 1918-
   Listening to the grass grow.
   A collection of the author's newspaper columns from
the Cherokee Scout.
   1. Meditations.   I. Cherokee scout.   II. Title.
BV4832.2.B254   1987   814'.54   87-30800
ISBN 0-9619190-0-0 (alk. paper)

DEDICATION

I lovingly dedicate this book to my grandchildren, and to my children who have been so eager to see, in book form, the many tales they listened to as youngsters.

ACKNOWLEDGEMENTS

Publishing a book is not an easy task—but, as demanding as it is, there *are* rewards. These rewards surface partially in the form of help, unsolicited and otherwise, from friends and associates who want the project to succeed. Following is an abbreviated recap of those whose efforts made *Listening to the Grass Grow* a reality. Many thanks to:

John and Kathi Boyle, whose encouragement and initial subvention spoke to their belief in the venture;

Bob Steed, whose advice, suggestions, and backliner note gave the book needed momentum;

Weaver Carringer, whose assistance throughout the compilation, publishing and promotion process was invaluable;

Ashby Cleary, whose judgment in the selection of columns for publication gave the book much of its personality;

Charles VanGorder, whose Prologue and many words of encouragement personified the true spirit of friendship that meant so much to Cuz before he died;

Nelle Bagley, whose countless errands and ideas became the glue that made the parts come together;

Mary Miller, whose proofreading, financial support, and ideas characterized her boundless generosity in this project as well as many others;

Christopher Bagley, whose literary talents expressed in his Epilogue would have made his Papa proud;

Irene Palmer, whose efficiency, follow-up, and supervision made *Listening to the Grass Grow* a quality product that was produced on schedule;

And, finally, to the many other friends, relatives, and business associates who offered words of support and encouragement. Without all these contributions, *Listening to the Grass Grow* would not have been possible.

Rick Bagley

TABLE OF CONTENTS

Dedication v
Acknowledgements vii
Table of Contents ix
Prologue xi

A Christmas to Remember 1
Bible Story 4
Joseph's Coat 7
Advocate of Public Health 9
Stupid Questions or Stupid Answers 16
We Did It Differently 19
Nero Brayed While the Preacher Burned 23
Pop Larkins 27
Wischief and the Outhouse Caper 30
First Sweetheart 35
The Cap'n Was My Buddy 38
Miscarriage of Justice 43
Order in the Court 46
Medicare's to Come Peticare Is Here 49
Willow Leg 53
Ellie-Pye 57
Boot Camp 63
Drawing Buckets 66
Semper Fidelis 69
The Glove Slap 73
Plans for a Slaying 77
Parris Island Rabbits 82

Meet John Glowa 86
Nemo the Beast 91
Day of Retribution 95
The Reunion 100
Tightening the Screws 105
I Get Mean 109
The Hurricane 113
After the Hurricane 117
Cuz May Turn to Widow Watching 122
The Immigrant 125
Happiness, Birds & Jacob 128
A Dry Eyed Funeral 131
A Place for Everything 134
Thanksgiving Cordial 137
Victim of Circumstances 141
Grandpa, Likker & Preachers 145
"Papa Neal" 148
Blind Date 153
Blue Stamps for Hung-Over Folks 156

    Cuz's Glossary 159
    Rick's Epilogue 161
    Christopher's Epilogue 162

PROLOGUE

When the black camel took Harry "Cuz" Bagley through the portals of the unseen curtain into eternity, it marked the termination of his earthly life on this planet, being the world as we know it.

It was the end of the worldly life of a great man of great character who had a deep respect for God—the Supreme Architect of the universe—a love for mankind, and a man with a great philosophy and many other facets of an altruistic integrity. At his death those of us who had the good fortune to know him personally seemed to feel the fracture of an important link in the contingent of the population around us. "Cuz" was a man who seemed to appreciate the gift of this life on earth. A man who never knew a stranger and always had a good word for everyone he had ever met, he possessed the ability to cheer up the downhearted and make one feel at ease.

He was a great family man and had a wide interest in civic, political and international affairs as well as a special interest in the people and customs in the mountainous area of Western North Carolina. To this latter he wrote a weekly column for a local newspaper, *The Cherokee Scout*. In these articles he would usually describe or allude to unusual characters, acquaintances, or conditions and colloquialisms of the region. In his writings he engaged his interesting philosophy embellished with a humorous touch that stimulated an eager desire to read the next week's column.

Very active in masonry in North Carolina, he was a member of Montgomery Lodge #426 AF&AM, a 32° Scottish Rite mason and a Shrine mason, A.A.O.N.M.S. of North America. During his sojourn in masonry, he noticed that there was not a specific jewel or apron for the District Deputy Grand Lecturer of the Grand Lodge of North Carolina to wear during the ceremonies. With this in mind he called upon his artistic ingenuity and designed a gem and apron later adopted by the Grand Lodge of N.C. to be worn by the Deputy Grand Lecturer in all master mason events.

"Cuz" was a deep, analytical and clear thinker which allowed him to keep well abreast of the times, especially current and past events. He had an agility with words which enabled him to express his thoughts enmeshed into beautiful word pictures in his weekly columns.

All of the above attributes suggested to those of us who knew "Cuz" well to concertedly join with his wife, Nelle, son Rick, and daughter Sharon in an effort to compile his essays into book form, thus preserving for those who had not known "Cuz" personally and for future generations to be able to enjoy his writings.

A thought (Author unknown):

"A Living Faith"
I've dreamed many dreams that never came true,
    I've seen them vanish at dawn,
    But I've realized enough of my dreams, thank God,
    To make me want to dream on.

                                  Charles O. Van Gorder, M.D.
                                       Andrews, North Carolina

A CHRISTMAS TO REMEMBER

For several weeks folks have been asking if I'm expecting a BIG Christmas. I tell them all the same thing, "No, I'm not. I'm just hoping for a happy one." Somehow I'm satisfied at Christmas time if the folks are all well and we can spend it together.

You see, along about this time every year I can't help but remember one particular Christmas that I had many, many years ago. That one came when I was twelve and it completely changed my outlook on every one since that date.

Those were the years of the Great Depression, and the hardships we knew during those years made an indelible impression on many a youngster, including me. We were fortunate in that we lived on a big farm where we were able to raise an abundance of good substantial food. This did get kinda coarse, now and then, but we never went hungry. I guess our biggest problem back then was keeping clothes fit to wear amongst folks.

I reckon every youngan generally has one certain, particular thing which he'd most like to find under the tree on Christmas morning. This particular Christmas I had my heart set on a pair of waterproof boots with a little pocket on the side for a knife. I had even torn out of the catalog the page on which was shown a picture of a pair like I wanted.

And every afternoon on my way home from school I would pass a store that had a pair exactly like my dream boots in the window. I am sure I wanted those boots more than anything I had ever heard of before. And I never overlooked an opportunity to haul that tattered page from the catalog out of my pocket to discuss with Mama and Papa the wonderful merits of a pair of boots like they were. When

I'd ask them if they thought, maybe, I would get them, they would invariably say, "I hope so," or "We'll see." I thought that I could never get their enthusiasm to equal mine. And it just seemed to me that I wanted those boots so badly that it would be criminal, almost, if I didn't get them. Finally the great day arrived, and I'm sure I heard the first rooster crow that morning. I made a bee-line for the Christmas tree. It took just a split second to realize that there were no boots under the tree.

Mama and Papa had both met me in there, and Mama had big tears rolling down her cheeks. And Papa looked as if he, too, could have shed a few without half trying. My disappointment was enormous, but I'm sure it was nothing to compare with theirs.

Mama put her arms around me and cried so hard and Papa came over and patted me on the shoulder and said, "Son, we sure wanted to get you those boots, but we just couldn't do it." Then Mama tried to explain about Evelyn not having any shoes, and about my still having a pretty good pair of brogans. Then she went on to tell me, trying to cheer me up, about Papa getting us a sack of flour and some chocolate and she said, "I'm going to bake us one of the biggest and best chocolate cakes for dinner today that you ever saw, and we're gonna have biscuits, too."

But I really wasn't interested in anything to eat and I didn't hang around to see my little sister open the box that had her brand new shoes inside. Nor was I interested in the new top or the little bitty sack of marbles with my name on them. As soon as I milked the cows and fed the other stock, I called my dog and we headed for the woods. Mama called and said, "Son, don't be late for dinner."

When I got back home, Mama told me to hurry and wash up so we could eat. She also told me that Buddy Larkin was gonna eat Christmas dinner with us. Buddy was the son of a neighbor who lived down the road a piece.

We all got to our places, sat down, and bowed our heads. and Papa prayed, "Lord, I feel mighty humble today, and I want to thank you for all you have done for me." Then Papa began listing many things that the Lord had done for us all. And, finally, he said, "And, Lord, I want to thank you for Mama here, and these children, and ask you for one more favor—Will you please, Lord, help me figure some way to get a pair of boots?"

Papa had a little more to talk to the Lord about, but I didn't hear what it was. I was sobbing.

When I had sat down and began listening to Papa's prayer, I thought about little Buddy Larkin sitting beside me. His mama had died just a few weeks before, and I remembered that his papa sometimes stayed away from home for several days at the time. And long before Papa said a word to the Lord about the boots that I hadn't gotten for Christmas, I was breaking to pieces inside.

As soon as Papa said, "Amen," I got up and hugged his neck and wept. Then I went to Mama and did the same thing. And I tried to tell them both how much they meant to me and just how UNIMPORTANT the boots really were.

I've never eaten a better Christmas dinner than Mama fixed that day, and I've never seen as many tears shed as we all did.

BIBLE STORY

"A prominent church lay worker said today that editorial writers and columnists should devote more space to Biblical stories." News item.

Maybe the fellow is right, so if you will turn with me to the 29th chapter of Genesis, we will proceed. The reason I'm asking you to read along with me is because there is a slight possibility that my interpretation of the events may not jibe with yours, and I most certainly do not want you to get the wrong impression of this particular Biblical story.

Jacob, the son of Isaac, headed east to make his fortune, and wound up at his Uncle Laban's house. Laban was the son of Nahor. When he got there he saw that his Uncle Laban was doing powerfully well and had a big flock of cows and sheep, and two daughters. The daughters were named Leah and Rachel. Well, this Rachel caught Jacob's eye right off the bat on account of she was very beautiful. The Bible didn't say much about how Leah looked except that she was "tender eyed." I reckon Jacob didn't care much for tender eyes, so he lit right in to courting Rachel.

Laban made him a proposition saying as how if Jacob would work for him seven years he could marry Rachel. Jacob was really sweet on Rachel so he took Laban up on the deal and for seven long years he labored for him. Finally, when the seven years were up, Laban threw a big wedding feast, and while the Good Book doesn't say so in so many words, it must have been a pretty wild sort of party and Jacob must have had a little too much to drink because the next morning when he woke up he found that he had been married to the tender eyed Leah. Naturally he was powerfully disappointed, and he was feeling pretty low on account of a hangover, so he strode up to old Laban and wanted to know what the score was.

Jacob said unto Laban, "Wherefore then hast thou beguiled me?" which was sure telling him off, and Laban, being pretty sharp, told Jacob that it was a custom in that land for the eldest daughter to be married before the youngest, although it was mighty strange that nothing had been said about it before then. Jacob was about to blow his top, but Laban came up with another proposition. He told Jacob that if he would work for him seven more years he could go ahead and marry Rachel. Jacob took him up on this deal and finally married Rachel, although I'm sure he was mighty cautious at the next wedding feast and stayed away from the punch bowl.

Years passed and Jacob wasn't getting anywhere. All he was doing was looking after Laban's sheep and cattle, so he went to Laban and said he had to have a raise. Laban asked him what he wanted and Jacob said he wanted all the cattle that were ringstreaked, speckled and spotted (Genesis 30:39) and Laban agreed to this, thinking as how there were not many that were ringstreaked, speckled and spotted.

Jacob was getting pretty smart, having been associated with Laban for fourteen years, and he figured a pretty sneaky way to get even with him.

What he did was to cut some green poplar, hazel and chestnut trees and cut the bark to make the white appear which left the branches looking sort of like stick candy, although that is not exactly the way it was described. (See Genesis 30:37.) He took the branches, placed them in the watering trough and when the Mama-cows-to-be came up to get water they saw the striped branches and they jumped back sudden like, thinking there were snakes in the watering trough and when the calves were born they were all ringstreaked. It wasn't long before Jacob had just about all of the strong cattle and old Laban was left with nothing but a bunch of worn out cows with their ribs showing. The 30th chapter winds up telling how Jacob prospered and had many maidservants, and manservants, and camels, and asses, plus a lot of striped cows.

Well, that's the way the story went, more or less, and I sure was pulling for Jacob to get even with the cunning Laban. It sort of reminded me of the Western TV shows which finally let the hero win out over the fellow with the beady eyes and curly mustache. I'll bet old Laban was beady eyed and had a mustache.

I hope this was what the church lay leader had in mind, and I'm mighty glad to cooperate with him in bringing you this Biblical story.

JOSEPH'S COAT

Maybe that church lay leader would prefer a story about Joseph, and here's how I have interpreted it.

This story about Joseph starts on page 48 of the Book of Genesis, in case you want to check me for accuracy. Joseph was 17 when the story started and he wore a loud sport coat. It was even louder than some of the sport coats worn today which have only three colors. Joseph's coat was of seven colors and it must have been a dandy. His brothers were very jealous on account of this sport coat and also because he was always having dreams which indicated he would some day be their lord and master. Dreams played a big part in the life of our hero. It seems that dreams back in those days were inspired from above. Nowadays they are caused from such things as hamburgers, beer and installment buying.

One day the brothers were out feeding their flocks and Joseph went looking for them. When they saw him coming they figured it was their chance to fix him good and proper. They first planned to slay him but later on decided to put him in a deep hole. About that time a bunch of Ishmeelites came by, so the brothers took Joseph out of this dry well and sold him for 20 pieces of silver which is about $2.00 in United States money, what with inflation and all. First, though, they slew a lamb and dipped Joseph's coat of seven colors. They never did kill anything much in the Bible. What they did was to slay things. And then they took the coat back to Jacob who figured something had sure et Joseph.

The Ishmeelites sold Joseph to a rich fellow in Egypt by the name of Potiphar and the first thing you know Joseph was just about running old Potiphar's business and everything was looking mighty good. About that time, though, Potiphar's wife took out after Joseph and she got mad because Joseph wouldn't have anything to do with her, so she told her husband a pack of lies and Joseph landed in the county jail. It was in this jail that Joseph got a chance to interpret some dreams. There was a lot of dreaming going on in the jail on account of the bad food and hard mattresses.

Later on King Pharoah started having nightmares, probably due to too much wine, and he got Joseph out of jail to interpret a dream about some kine and ears of corn. Joseph hit the dreams right on the head, predicting seven years of famine. Pharoah made him Secretary of Agriculture, Secretary of Commerce (Joseph sure knew how to trade), Secretary of State, and he would have made him Secretary of Health, Education and Welfare but he learned that Joseph couldn't use the typewriter. During the bumper crop years they stored all the surplus instead of using the allotment plan and when the seven lean years came they had more corn and stuff than you could shake a stick at.

In the meantime, Joseph's mean brothers were getting powerful hungry and when they heard about all the corn in Egypt they set out to buy up some. They didn't recognize Joseph and he had a good time getting even with em for messing up his sport coat. Finally, though, he not only gave them all the grain they could haul off, but he gave their money back, which is the first instance we have of politicians helping out their kinfolks at the expense of the government. Everything worked out swell as far as I read. They had a family reunion and they kissed and had a good time. Pharoah let em have a plantation in Goshen, also at government expense. Looking back, if the brethren hadn't sold Joseph into slavery the whole shooting match would have starved to death during the seven lean years. The moral of the story is that if you can get two bucks for your little brother, let him go.

The above is the reason I do not write much about the Bible.

ADVOCATE OF PUBLIC HEALTH

My concern for public health began at a very early age. In fact, I was only in the fifth grade when the incident occurred which proves that I was a staunch supporter of the matter.

It all began with a bright and warm sunny Saturday morning down in East Brewton, Alabama. I had tended to a few small chores around the house when I realized that if I didn't get gone some place that Mama would soon have me wasting a lot of mighty valuable time doing some others.

I requested, and was granted, permission to go off in the woods behind the house to see if I could, maybe, kill a few jay birds. Those pesky things were powerful bad to eat the figs right off the trees before they were anything like ready to be preserved. Besides the figs, they'd also play havoc with strawberries and just about any other kind of fruit.

Before I left to hunt I went out to the edge of the gravel road in front of our house and filled my pockets with small rocks, just the right size to fit my slingshot which was my weapon. And I might add that it was made out of red inner-tube which was the best kind.

I did go through those woods and I did shoot at a couple or three jay birds, a woodpecker or two, and one yellowhammer. I didn't kill any of em on account of I reckon I was in too big of a hurry to get to Jake Scott's house, and on top of that I wasn't taking "dead aim."

I made it to Jake's in nothing flat and after a hurried discussion with him we concocted some wild yarn to get him away from his house. We had to slip off from Ed Neal and Aubrey, two of his little brothers, on account of we didn't figure they were old enough to go with us, their being only in the fourth and second grades. We were fearful for their well-being.

Next we managed to get Claudis Beasley and Potlicker Capps to join us. That was our gang. I mean GROUP.

We headed for another patch of woods, made a wide circle and came into the clearing behind the schoolhouse. We fooled around the school yard for a little while, and I noticed that a window had been left open on the ground floor. The building was a two-story with a full basement which made what we called the ground floor a pretty good distance from the ground. None of us could anywheres near reach that open window. And we all agreed that we should get into that building and inspect it.

The focal point of our interest was our own classroom.

Our problem of actually making it into the building was soon solved by our sending Potlicker back to his house for an ax. The reason he was elected for this was on account of he lived the nearest to the school and it would be no problem for him to sneak back to the backside of his house where their wood pile was, pick up their ax, and scamper back to where the action was.

In no time a tall he was back and we chopped down a small pine sapling which we placed on the bottom of the open window, and it wasn't a bit of trouble for us to climb that and get into the building.

This all happened before our school had any in-door plumbing. There were just two little shacks away out back of the schoolhouse, one for the boys and the other for the girls . . . as you probably suspected.

We had a teacher who was a very tall and large lady. She would not tolerate any monkey business in her class and for the least little ole thing she would jerk any youngan out of his or her seat up to the front of the room and wear em out properly. This applied to everybody in her class and we had some great big ole boys, too, on account of some of em didn't get started to school when they were six years old. I'll tell you this lady was big enough to go bear hunting with a switch.

Our room was on the top floor of the building and it had two "L" shaped cloak rooms which amounted to placing teacher's desk about in the middle of the "U" formed by the two L's. There was a partition between the two rooms. One was a cloak room for us youngans where we hung our sweaters and left our lunches. The other cloak room belonged to Miss Furnell and on the very first day of school that year she had sternly admonished us that her cloak room was strictly OFF-LIMITS to us. And, if she were EVER to catch any of us in there she would slap tear us up. We purely did believe her.

I mentioned those two little shacks out behind the schoolhouse. As you might well imagine it was necessary to raise our hands several times a day to "be excused." However, she strongly encouraged that these matters be attended to during recess, lunch period, and play period. If she thought we were asking to be excused too often she would send another youngan after us. Sometimes she would just holler out the window and tell us that we'd better get back in the room.

Now, we hadn't been going to school but a few days before we noticed that Miss Furnell never left the room. Well, she did, too, on rare occasions when she had to go to the principal's office or some place in the building itself. When she did leave the room, we'd sneaked a few peeks out the back window and she NEVER EVER was seen heading to the little girl's outhouse. Any time she ever did leave the room she would always leave some little old tattle-tale to write the names down of those of us who even so much as whispered.

Another item that we noticed was that several times a day she would leave her desk and go into her cloak room. In a hurry we learned that we weren't safe even with her in there on account of she could hear everything that went on while she was in there and on several occasions came out to thrash whoever made a sound while she was in seclusion.

So, I reckon it was kindly natural for us to have some curiosity about her cloak room. That's why, when we spotted that open window, we felt compelled to enter and make an inspection.

What a revelation that was!

The very first thing we discovered—well, there wasn't a way on earth that we could have missed finding 41 half-gallon fruit jars neatly lined up along the short end of the "L" of her cloak room. Then, in addition, there were five or six unopened cases of jars stacked one atop another. All brand new jars. Ready for canning or whatever.

Uh, I mean UGH, the 41 jars neatly aligned along the wall were all filled to capacity with, uh—with a most easily recognizable liquid. And even though each jar had its lid tightly closed, the odor was sumpin fierce. I'm here to tell you . . . It was a pure mystery to us how we had not ever noticed that odor before. Still, I suppose a body can sort of get accustomed to most anything like that if subjected to it very gradually.

Being so civical minded as I was at that time, the very first thought I had and voiced to my colleagues was sumpin about we, as well as all our classmates, were being exposed to a mighty terrible health hazard.

On second thought I kindly remember that we all sort of simultaneously roared something about—well, "Now we know how come the old witch (I'm not sure we spelled that right) never left the room to go to the shed house."

In nothing flat Potlicker suggested that we empty all of her jars. Said sumpin about how surprised she'd be when she got back on Monday morning and saw em all ready to go again.

We went along with Potlicker's plan. To start with. We opened the hollering window and very, very carefully removed all the lids— one at a time, though, just one at a time on account of we sure didn't want any accidents happening to us, like maybe getting some of it on us. And if you know ANYTHING about that stuff, when properly aged—we'd never have gotten rid of that STINK.

No need to tell you that it didn't take four eager boys long to empty 41 jars out that window. What a stinking, big mess that did make in our schoolyard and right under our classroom window too.

Some time during the emptying process I suggested that we take all those jars down to a small creek very near the edge of the school yard and use em for target practice with our slingshots. My collaborators thought that was the finest idea we'd had all morning.

However, in following this brilliant plan, it necessitated our replacing all the jar lids, getting em downstairs to our port of entry, or, you know, to the window where our pole was.

In drawing straws I was one of the losers so Jake, Potlicker, and I climbed down the pole to the ground and Claudis gently dropped them down to us. Amazingly enough we were able to get em all down without breaking a single one. However, in spite of all we could do there were a few drops of the stuff that got on all of us. We decided that we'd just HAVE TO stand it. We told each other we'd wash it off when we got to the creek.

Sometime before we'd gotten all 41 jars down safely on the ground, Jake suggested that we should go back to our beloved teacher's cloak room and get all those boxes of empty jars. In other words, he thought it would be just great to slap clean the old gal out complete. After all, he just didn't think that 41 jars would give us enough target practice.

Of course, we all agreed with him and the three of us "ground boys" scampered back up that pole and hot-footed it back and brought down all the rest of her storage supply. My, oh my. What fun we had!

We had to drop each of these jars down individually too on account of we were afraid that if we dropped a whole box at once we might break em and we certainly didn't want that to happen until we were good and ready.

It took us a while to get every last one of those half-gallon fruit jars down to the creek. But before we left the school house, we removed our pole, closed both windows, and made sure that our tracks were erased.

We took care of that track business by using the limbs cut from our pine sapling and sweeping a good portion of the school yard. And then the Good Lord was on our side all the way on account of He sent us a gully-busting rain that afternoon which would have erased the tracks of a bulldozer.

We lined all those jars up along the edge of the creek and took turns shooting at em. All the time we were talking about how eager we were for school to take in on Monday morning. I'm telling you, none of us could hardly wait.

Before we parted that day about noon we swore each other to secrecy. Crossed our hearts and hoped to die, each ten times, if we so much as uttered the first word to a living soul about the incident. We all felt very confident on account of we knew that if SHE ever found out that she would slap kill us stone-cold, grave-yard dead.

That was the longest weekend I can ever remember spending. Just waiting for Monday morning.

Finally, it did get to East Brewton, Alabama and our schoolhouse and we four boys were the first ones in our room after the bell rang.

Miss Furnell came in last and closed the door, got out her roll book, and called the roll.

Now usually it'd take about an hour to get ready to go to her cloak room. That was the longest hour I ever lived and none of us boys dared look at one another. We were too busy studying. I mean we's a bearing down on it.

Finally we heard Miss Furnell ease her chair back. The four of us were holding our books so that we didn't even have to take em down from in front of our faces to watch her. It was her usual time. She headed for her cloak room, went inside, stayed about eight or ten seconds and came back and sat down. In just about five more minutes she got up and went back in there. This time she didn't stay so long.

When she came out she stood in front of the class with her hands on her massive hips and glared at us over the top of her glasses. I'm absolutely positive that no bunch of youngans ever got glared at as hard as she laid it on us that morning. I was sweating sumpin awful and I found out later that my buddies were too. The stuff was dripping off the end of my nose but I didn't dare make a move to wipe it off. No Siree!

Finally, and it seemed like hours, but I'm sure it couldn't have been more than a couple of minutes, but FINALLY that old gal HAD TO GO. Whereupon she turned on her heel and lit a shuck out of that room and we could hear her fairly running down those stairs. In a minute or so one of the innocent children, a little girl, and I'll never ever forget her name, Mary Clayton, said out loud, "I wonder where Miss Furnell has gone." The reason Mary even so much as opened her mouth was on account of our teacher was in such a hurry that she didn't remember to appoint a tattletale—I mean monitor—before she left the room.

Mary must have suspected sumpin. She was sitting in the back of the room and she got out of her seat and said, "Yawl come look at Miss Furnell go!" Every youngan in that room was up and looking out that window in a flash.

We could see the ole girl walking mighty fast toward the you know what. Then she began to run. All of a sudden she stopped dead still in her tracks, and from there on she walked with very, very short steps on to the little girls' outhouse. It was our united opinion that she lacked just a few steps getting there in time.

She stayed a right smart little while. When she returned to the room we were all studying as hard as we could.

There was never a word said about that episode until a couple of years later when this teacher left our school and went to another state to teach. Even the youngans in our class wanted to give us the keys to the playground.

STUPID QUESTIONS OR STUPID ANSWERS???

Americans are supposed to be the best informed people in the world and if we are, then I'm kinda sorry for some of the other folks.

In my work I meet all kinds of people and I try to treat each one of them as courteously as I know how. I do my best to answer all their questions intelligently and in language they can understand. However, I'm just not prepared for the questions I sometimes get.

I realize that everyone isn't up on the subjects of dams, steam plants, kilowatts, and things like that as those of us who have worked in and around them for years. And I guess I would probably ask silly questions too if I were being shown around Cape Kennedy, for instance. However, I have had some unusual ones tossed my way over the years.

One day I was talking to a group out in front of the powerhouse; they were looking at the turbulent water as it boiled up in the tailrace. It was early in the spring and the water was still muddy. One gentleman asked, "You get a lot more electricity out of the water when it's muddy, don't you?"

Well, it took me several minutes to explain that whether the water was muddy or clear had nothing to do with how much electricity we could generate. I said I explained to him about that; what I should have said was that I tried. I think I only confused him. In fact, I am pretty sure I did cause in laboring with his question I got kinda confused myself. Before it was over I was sorry I hadn't just told him, "Yes sir," in answer to his question.

I was showing another group of people a schematic diagram of TVA's water control system. Now this is a sort of map showing all the dams in the system and their respective locations on the different rivers. I had told them that after the water was released here at Hiwassee Dam it flowed on down river and generated power at eight more dams. An intelligent looking lady spoke up very indignantly, "Well, I thought these TVA dams were more efficient than that!" Then I had to ask what she meant. She said it looked mighty inefficient to her for us not to get all the electricity out of the water the first time we fooled with it. I kept calm. I always try to keep calm. Before I could get an edge in word-wise she was gonna contact her congressman about the gross inefficiency of TVA's dams.

After she sorta simmered down a little I began trying to explain. What I had in mind to explain was that there was no electricity in the water. And all that about its merely supplying the power to turn the turbine which in turn spun the generator and the rest of the story.

I got exactly no where. She wasn't having any part of it and accused me of just trying to "cover up" for TVA. What I was really trying to do was UNCOVER for TVA. The pamphlets I'd given her when the group came in, she disgustedly tossed over on the desk on her way out.

Now that particular remark about the water generating power so many times after it left Hiwassee, I guess I'd gotten away with for at least a thousand times before. But not on that day. I'll bet she gave her pore congressman down the country about that.

Then one day a fellow asked how we managed to get the electricity into them little hollow wires. Hollow wires? I told him they weren't and he wanted to know how the heck we ever managed to get the stuff to travel through the wires if they weren't hollow. As usual I tried to explain. I am a big dope. I should just have told him we used little bitty funnels to get it into them hollow wires and that compressed air then pushed it where it was going.

Another one wanted to know if we stored the electricity in those big tanks out in the switchyard. I had a good time with this one too.

I have had many such interesting questions, but I reckon the best of all was the one a well-dressed, apparently intelligent, gentleman asked. He wanted to know which direction this river flowed before the dam was built.

You think these folks are ignorant? Well, they weren't. At least not like some of my kinfolks.

Not long ago I was visiting an aunt of mine (by marriage, thank goodness—and I'm sorry too) and in a discussion I happened to mention something about the South having lost the Civil War. And, man, she was up in arms! She honestly believes that we had clobbered them Yankees. You probably think she was real ignorant but she ain't. Why I don't even know who won the Korean War. Do you?

WE DID IT DIFFERENTLY

A few years ago the son of friends of ours had his current girl friend's name on a tag and put it on his car. I saw it and it caused me to do some reflecting about how we boys used to sorta advertise our attachment to the fairer sex. We would never have even considered doing such a thing as putting her name or initials on a car. Reason we wouldn't have was on account of we just didn't have any cars. That took care of that.

The way we handled it was like this, and I think that our plan was far more durable: We carved our initials and our girl's on trees. Occasionally we'd even do a little carving on a desk in the school room. However, this was frowned on by some of our teachers. Durn near all of them, in fact. But they seldom said very much about the initial carving we did on the trees, that is, unless we began whittling them down too close to the edge of the school yard.

Now anytime we saw one of our buddies behind a tree we knew automatically that, well, first of all, we knew that he wasn't doing what you're thinking, in case you're thinking THAT—we knew he was just busy whittling his and her initials on the tree.

Several of us had to do an awful lot of whittling. Me especially, because it just seemed like I had bad luck with my girls. They sure were fickle. And it was their fickleness that caused me to have to do so much whittling. Besides having to whittle a new girl's initials pretty often I also felt like it served the latest lassie just right when I went back and whittled off her initials. That was usually harder to do than the original whittling.

I never will forget that one gal that threw me over so unceremoniously. I really fixed her. What I did was I rode my horse into town one Saturday morning and took a hatchet along with me and, I'm telling you, I made quick work of getting her whittled out. I AXED her off that tree. And alongside our initials I had carved a couple of hearts with arrows through them and the word, Love. It was just about the most artistic job I ever turned out and then to have it end like it did was enough to make a fellow's blood boil.

I'm even sorry I so much as thought of her. And to put her and me on that tree took me four play periods and five recesses. But it sure didn't take me that long to lay the ax to her. Tell you the truth, she was lucky I did my hatchet work on that water oak instead of her.

But then came along a young lady by the name of Nellie O'Neal. Oh, she didn't just "come along;" she was there all the time. It was just that it was some time before I began noticing her.

And almost from the beginning I started studying about how our initials would look on the side of some big water oak. The reason I usually used water oaks for this sort of thing was because the bark on them was smoother, easier to work. Poplars were all right, sweetgums, too, but they grew too fast and in a few years they'd outgrown your art work.

Anyhow I visualized HCB & NO, maybe with some more hearts and arrows and stuff. Then, finally, when things progressed far enough along—well, she let me walk her home from school—I could hardly wait to get our initials on several trees, a desk or two, and all my books.

On one particular big oak near the school yard I carved a tremendous HCB & NO. And when I got it all done, somehow or other that just didn't look balanced. You see, she had only two initials and I had three. I pondered over this for a while and then decided that I had to do something about that. Besides the lack of balance there, her initials spelled the word "NO" and I purely didn't like the looks of that. Yeah, even though she was all the time saying no about first one thing and then another.

I concluded that this situation demanded some positive action. So, I added a "B" to her initials. That was THE answer. Now it was all balanced and everything. HCB & NOB. Hearts and arrows, love, flowers, and stuff. Man, what a masterful job that really was. I guessed that I had done the best on that one of any I'd ever carved. And besides, I had plans for changing her No to a Yes, and with those plans I considered that adding that "B" was exactly right.

Well sir, it was dead right. I married the gal.

You know I never could get her anything like interested in going with me to let me show her all that. What she said was something about she wasn't about to go to the woods with me.

Then years afterward we were down home and just for the heck of it I drove over to the old schoolhouse which, incidently, is still in use and is now known as The Church Street School in Andalusia, Alabama.

I was feeling sorta nostalgic so I just parked in front of the schoolhouse and walked around it, and I was reminiscing a mile a minute. That big water oak was still there so I checked on it, and there, big as life, was my art work still intact. My pulse picked up a beat or two. But on close inspection I noticed that some cotton picking, chicken plucking, apple knocking jerk had done some carving of his own. My middle initial "C" had been changed to an "O" and then, you see, it all turned out to be just plain ole HOB—NOB.

I was sure sore about that. And because somebody messed that up, I just hope that, whoever it was, they didn't amount to anything either.

Just like me.

NERO BRAYED WHILE THE PREACHER BURNED

Everybody said that we had the meanest, fightingest, brayingest mule of anybody who went to our church. They were right.

Have you ever heard of anybody being ashamed of a mule? Mama always said that she had never, in her whole life, been so ashamed of anything as she was of old Nero, our mean braying mule. And she was continually onto Papa to get rid of that ornery beast. He finally did but not before Nero had made himself quite a reputation and turned nearly everybody in the whole church against us.

It seemed that every time we took a notion to go to church that would be the very time that Nero would pick to show out the most. And Mama would always tell Papa that that was the very last time she intended to go to church until he got shed of that awful mule. Papa would always chuckle, slap Nero lightly with the lines and tell her, "There's one thing you can sure say for this mule and that is he's got spirit." Mama'd say, "It's demons he's got if anything."

We would skip going to church a Sunday or two, then Mama would decide that we just had to go back. She would say, "I'll be doggoned if just one mean mule is gonna keep me and my family away from the Lord's house." And back we would go for another whack at it with Nero.

The way he first began to disturb the public worship was with his braying. He'd bray longer and louder than anybody else's mule in that church yard. If he had been born a human, I'm pretty sure he would have been a song leader, and a darn good one too on account of when he commenced he wouldn't stop until he had all the jackasses in the whole churchyard a-singing the blues.

He got so bad that finally Preacher Snyder and a committee came to see Papa and they asked him if there wasn't something he could do about that cussed mule.

When Papa found out why they had come he was tickled. He said that he reckoned that was the first time in history a delegation from any church ever had to go see a brother about the conduct of a mule. Mama said she was mortified, my sisters said they didn't believe they could stand it, but Ray was too little to care one way or the other. Papa and I were just plain tickled. Actually we were kinda proud of old Nero and said as much, at least Papa did. I just agreed with him but Mama said, "It's just like you two to think it's funny. You've both got a great big devilish streak in you."

We missed church for two or three Sundays after the parson and the deacons met with Papa about our mule, but then Mama couldn't stand it any longer; she decided we just had to get back. Before we braved our ordeal again, though, she and Papa concluded that it just might be a good idea if I stayed outside with Nero to kindly keep him quiet. I was supposed to swarp him with a big switch every time he got ready to hee-haw.

When I found out about my new ecclesiastical duties—getting to stay outside to mind that mule—why, I figgered he was just about the finest mule anywhere on that side of Missouri.

My first Sunday on duty with Nero I did such a fine job that Mama, Papa, Preacher Snyder, and half the congregation were patting me on the back. I was sure that I had found my life's calling and had a job that was a lot more exciting than sitting through long sieges of mighty dry preaching.

The next Sunday, though, I had a little trouble. I had persuaded Jake Scott and Claude Beasley to stay outside and help me look after Nero. They did. So, we got to shooting jaybirds with our slingshots, you know, to have something to do while Nero was behaving. We got kinda busy with this project and before we knew it, he commenced.

We were too far from him to swarp him so I told my buddies we'd just shoot him with our slingshots and we did. You know how a flat rock will sorta sail when you throw or shoot it? This one did just like that.

Now you wouldn't think that anybody could miss as big a target as a mule, but on account of that flat rock I sure did. But not much.

That durn rock sailed right past Nero and busted out a big windowpane right beside where Mama and Papa, Ray, and the girls were sitting.

Preacher Snyder stopped, Papa said, right in the middle of a long prayer and looked right straight at him. Papa just excused himself and came outside and tore me up. Then he went back inside.

For the next few Sundays us boys didn't do anything much but just play marbles and mumblety-peg right there close where we could knock the H., uh, where we could knock the stuffing out of that ole mule. Then I was pretty certain I had broken him of his bad habit, so my helpers and I decided we could maybe risk slipping off down to the spring while Nero wasn't looking.

We must have stayed a little longer than we figured. I heard the low-down rascal beller. Sounded like he was a way off. We hightailed it back to the churchyard, but it was already too late.

Nero had somehow gotten loose and, Papa told me later, he had come and stuck his old head in the window right behind the pulpit and brayed the darnedest racket he had ever brayed in his life. Papa said Preacher Snyder yelled, "AMEN, and Lord help us!" Then Papa said he hit old Nero up side the head with one of our new Stamps-Baxter song books and the meetin' was over for that Sunday.

After Papa hit old Nero he—Nero, not Papa—went biting and kicking through that bunch of mules and horses in the churchyard, several of them broke loose, and we and three other families had to walk home from church.

Mama was more than humiliated this time. She was mad at Papa, me, my buddies, as well as pore old Nero. I don't think it was so much what all Mama had to say as it was that three-mile walk home in the hot July sun that convinced Papa he would sure have to trade Nero off. I certainly did hate to see him go. It was sorta like losing a member of the family.

POP LARKINS

If there was ever a natural born comedian, Pop Larkins was. I met him in the old Moore General V. A. Hospital at Swannanoa, N. C. shortly after WWII when we were both patients there.

WW I was Pop's war, during the course of which he lost his right foot at the ankle. He had turned in to the hospital to get a new artificial foot. While he was waiting, the V. A. was pulling his teeth to fit him with sto-boughten ones.

Pop was anxious to get off on the right foot as he came into the ward, and I can tell you for sure he knew just the lick it was done by.

Some time, some where, before he actually got into the ward, he stopped and put his artificial foot on so that the toe pointed backward. Then he sorta waltzed into where the rest of us were—with his toes pointing both for'n aft.

From the way he walked you couldn't tell that he wasn't just born that way. He went to each occupied bed in the ward and introduced himself: "I'm Pop Larkins from Forest City." Then he would reach into a bulging side-pocket of his tattered and mismatched suit coat and pull out a piece of homemade twist tobacco and ask, "Would ye'ns keer for a little tweest?"

Well, he hadn't been in the ward five minutes before every man in there knew who he was, where he was from, several things about his family, and how he made his living. He told us that he sure wouldn't want it "no-rated around" but about all he had ever done was make and sell bootleg licker, raise and fight game chickens, possum hunt, and, he added, "I used to gamble a little now and agin."

We asked him if the revenoors had ever caught him. He said, "Oh, I've been ketched a time or two, but I ain't never had to do no time. Why, whenever I had to actual go to the big court, I'd allus take off this here ole foot and go before the jedge on my homemade crutches, in the raggediest ole overhauls I had. An ye know whut, I jes don't bleave there's no jedge in these hills that'd send a pitiful looking critter like me to the road for making a leetle licker."

He gave his feet credit for "not getting ketched no more'n I did." It seemed that he'd driven a lot of revenoors just about nutty when they began trying to track him. He said, "Now you jist imagine how baffling hit'd be to come up on a set of tracks like mine in the snow. Whichaways would ye'ns go a looking fer me?"

Pop could talk and take care of the biggest cud of homemade twist that I ever saw. As his stories progressed, he would get excited, just as if the revenoors were actually breathing down his collar, and as his excitement grew, he had to shift that wad of twist more and more often from jaw to jaw.

Between his stories and his gymnastics with his chewing tobacco, he kept his audience spellbound. And worried! We were always afraid that he would either strangle to death or maybe give us all an amber juice shower. Neither ever happened.

He never finished a yarn without having us all busting our sides laughing at him. Then when we were all in an uproar, he would get up, go to his bed, get his can, and spit what looked like about a quart.

Pop said they had him in the big court one time that he would never forget. "The jedge," he said, "kept a asting me reckin how much licker I'd made in my whole life. He said, reckin a 100,000 gallons? I told him I never knowed. Finally he ast me, 'Pop, reckin you've made this court-room full?' And I said, 'Jedge, yo honah, I don't know if I've made her full er not, but I'm purty shore I've made enough to make er slosh.' " Pop said that ole judge had one more time trying to quieten everybody down.

Pop couldn't read and write so he had to have a secretary, he told us. I volunteered right quick for the job. Since this service was so readily available and "free fer nothing," as Pop said, he wanted a letter written to that "leetle woman," Maw Larkins, about every other day. So he dictated and I wrote, only I seldom wrote exactly what he dictated. What I did mostly was write Maw Larkins some powerful love letters—torrid, tender, and affectionate.

Now Maw could read and write, and she got mighty curious right quick about what kind of wonderful drugs they were giving Pop and what they were feeding him. She would remind him of his age, etc., but, take it altogether, she seemed powerful pleased with this miraculous transformation in Pop. Time and again she invited him to come home for "leastways a day or two."

Finally when Pop failed to accept her urgent invitation, she paid him an un-announced visit one day at lunch time. Pop had finished his lunch and was sitting out on the sun porch on a glider. A nurse's aide who had served our trays and was waiting for us to eat before picking them up was sitting on the opposite end of the glider, about six feet from Pop. She was reading her paper, unaware I think, of his even being on the porch. I know she was absolutely unaware of an approaching storm in the person of one little bitty dried up Maw Larkins.

Maw exploded onto that sun porch and screamed, "There ye air!" as she landed a haymaker to pore ole Pop's ear, "jist whir I figgered ye'd be. Ye hain't fit fer nothing but to lay around these ole GIVERMINT HOSSPITTALS and talk to the wimmen!"

The nurse's aide left that sun porch like something was after her. And in a few seconds Pop and Maw walked back together through the ward. He had his arm around her waist. I said to him. "Pop, she nearly knocked your head off, didn't she?" He said, "Nah, twarn't nothing but a love tap."

Needless to say we all hated to see Pop get all fixed up and go home. He was the best medicine any of us had ever had. Before he left we made up a little pot and bought him a completely new outfit from top to bottom. He modeled them for us. He said, "Boys, I'm glad yawl like the way I look, but, shore nuff, I can't wear a git up like this to Forest City. Why, iffen I did, they'd arrest me fore I got acrost the street." Then he went on to tell us that it was "sich a nice looking outfit that I reckin Maw'll want me to save it to be laid out in."

Then he came to each of us and shook hands and wished us well and told us goodbye. There wasn't a dry eye in the house as the old man turned his back and left, with both feet pointing in the same direction.

WISCHIEF AND THE OUTHOUSE CAPER

Wischief is a noun and I reckon it is about the most unusual one of the whole bunch on account of it has a right smart of tense connected with it. Now I don't mean tenses like present, past, and future. I'm talking about the kind that resembles nervousness, things like that. As for wischief, you need not look it up because, so far, none of the dictionary manufacturers have come across it. Maybe it's like the word "ain't." You know there was a long time before any of them would even admit that there was such a word.

Wischief means wishing one could get into some mischief. Actually, this is a kind of psychological affliction from which I suffered a whole lot while I was trying to grow up. Well, I don't suppose that it is quite accurate to say that I really suffered from it. I just had to contend with it right muchly years ago. And, tell you the truth, ever since I managed to get grown I have had slight recurrences of the malady.

The Byrds, for example. I got along just fine with the Byrd boys because they were near my age and many times they would help me out with the stuff I thought up, but the rest of the family thought and said that a mean boy like I was ought to be sent off somewhere.

I won't ever forget one particular Easter Sunday down home. Folks were just like they are now. They might miss church and Sunday school for a solid year but come Easter they would dress up in their best finery and would somehow manage to make it to services.

Every last one of the Byrds came that day. In fact, they were already there when we drove up. And as soon as I saw them I began having a real bad case of wischief. I was afraid to even look at Mama because I was just sure that she'd extract some kind of promise from me about behaving myself. But I didn't have to look at her that day. Even before we got out of the wagon, she turned around to me and said, "Now, young man, you better behave yourself here today or I'll wear you out good and proper when I get you home."

I told her, "Yes,'m." And Papa added, "Son, you'd better listen to your Mama." I told him, "Yessir."

So that pretty well took care of anything I might be able to think up to do while we were actually there at church. But I noticed that neither of them mentioned anything about behaving myself the rest of that whole day—it was just CHURCH. I felt a right smart better when I began to study about how the balance of the day could be used, maybe.

I was giving the problem a lot of serious thought until Preacher Willis began preaching about a fellow by the name of Daniel somehow getting into that terrible lion's den. He soon preached him safely out of that trouble and I went back to work on my own project.

Long before Preacher Willis ever got through relating the two events of Daniel in the lion's den and the Good Lord's rising from the dead I had a plan.

Soon as the congregation was dismissed I ask Papa if I could take the short cut through the woods and not ride with em back home. He readily agreed and so did Mama. I told em I wanted to see if I could beat em home. I knew I could. In fact if I hadn't known that, I wouldn't have had a chance to do what I had in mind.

Mama warned me to go straight home. I promised that I sure would. And I did. As hard as I could. As soon as I got there I got Papa's claw hammer and a handful of the biggest nails I could find and headed for our dear friend the Byrd's house.

Yep, I had some carpenter work planned but not on their dwelling house. It was another structure that I had in mind.

You see, back in those days very few folks had any indoor plumbing and absolutely no country folks had it. And the Byrds and we certainly were country folks. About as country as anybody could get.

Maybe you have already imagined what I did but in case you haven't I'll go into a little more details.

The Byrds had a very elaborate outhouse. It had a compartment for ladies and one for gentlemen. And each compartment had accommodations for two at a time. I am sure that you can visualize the many advantages such a structure would have over every other outhouse in our community. Besides all that, it was brand new and I'm sure they took an awful lot of pride in it. Tell you the truth, that thing was the talk of the neighborhood. Nobody had anything to compare with it.

They were so proud of it that they built the thing where it could be easily seen from the road. There weren't any trees around anywhere close; there just wasn't anything to keep any and EVERYBODY from seeing the Byrd's Big John.

Well, first of all, I went into each of the little rooms and collected the catalogs and put them on the outside. Then I nailed the lids down on the uh—well, you know each of those places had a lid and I nailed em down extry good. Then I nailed the doors shut with the very biggest nails I had and headed for home. About half way home I left their catalogs in some tall weeds.

Soon as I got safely back on our property I climbed up into a big pecan tree that afforded an excellent view of the entire countryside, and especially the Byrd's house.

I didn't have long to wait. They all got back home much sooner than I had expected and, Lo and Behold, they had brought company home with em for Easter Sunday Dinner! I certainly did admire their neighborliness. What I really figured was that the only reason they had invited this company was on account of their having such a fancy new building on their property. I'll tell you I just didn't give them Byrds credit for much.

Business picked up very sharply there in just a minute or two. Since Mrs. Byrd and her lady friend were gonna have to fix dinner they went first. They were in sort of a hurry. Mrs. Byrd made a fast retreat toward the barn and I'm pretty sure she told Mr. Byrd about the situation. In no time a tall he was out there to remedy things. But he just had his hammer. That wasn't enough. Next he attacked the doors with a crowbar. That got em open and he headed back for the barn to finish unhitching and feeding his and his friend's mules.

He didn't make it all the way back though before Mrs. Byrd had called him back to the John. You know, to get the lids open. Well sir, all this took a good deal of time and before everything was taken care of, everyone of the Byrds were out in the yard to see what was happening. And all their company.

Finally the ladies got inside again but only I knew that they'd be heard from again in just a little bit. In no time I saw Mrs. Byrd stick her head out of the door and yell for one of her daughters. Daughter made a quick trip to see what else was wrong. Then she had to go back in the house. It took her a while to find new catalogs.

I didn't get to talk with the Byrd boys for two or three days but when I did that was something else. We all wondered who in the world would have ever thought up such a thing. And they told me, too, that their papa had done some of the finest cussin' that they had ever heard in all their born days.

FIRST SWEETHEART

A few years ago I got to rambling around down in south Alabama, and a thing happened that I think I should tell you about. Actually I feel sort of burdened about it, like maybe I should pass along some advice to you men folks, especially. And if there are any of you women who don't enjoy reading advice for the old man, then don't you read this. You just read the Of Interest To Women page.

However, this will be such good advice maybe you ought to go ahead and read it so you can tell your husband what I said just in case he doesn't read it.

While I was traipsing around down in Alabama, I had to go through a little town where the parents of my very first sweetheart lived. I just thought I would look them up though I had had a grudge against em for a pretty long time. This grudge I had was because I wanted to marry their daughter when I was fifteen and they said, "NO!"

Anyhow I had forgiven them for that and hunted them up. It took some doing but I finally found their house and knocked on the door. Had to knock several times, pretty hard. I remembered that Sweetheart's daddy was hard of hearing even when I had first known him. Eventually I heard him coming—but it wasn't him. It was a HER and I hadn't ever seen this particular HER before in my life I didn't think. I knew it couldn't be his wife on account of she was a lot bigger than he was. This woman was all shriveled plumb up to nothing.

Since I didn't know who she was I asked if Mr. Bones was at home and if I could see him. She assured me that he was and I could. As soon as she began telling me where he was I realized who SHE was. You guessed it. Of course, she was Sally Kate! My very first Sweetheart. And you know what I did as soon as I knew it was her? I forgave her mama and papa all over again for having refused to let me marry her years and years ago. And just for good measure I forgave them several more times while I was there. I'll tell you, Old Father Time had shore been rough on Sally Kate.

She explained that, "Papa is out in the garden and I'll go tell him that you would like to see him." Then she asked, "Who shall I tell him is asking for him?" You see she never recognized me a tall! That nearly killed my pride too. And because she had done such a good job of forgetting all about me I forgave her parents again.

I said to her, "Aw, you know who I am, Mam." She took a long hard look at me and assured me that if she had ever seen me before in her life that she most assuredly did not remember who I was. That kinda stung me. Then she wanted to know where I was from. When I told her, "North Carolina," she wasn't satisfied and strode out to take a long look at the tag on my car. Even though it matched what I had told her, she said that that didn't help her any with trying to place me. I forgave her folks one more time.

She asked me to take my hat off. You see I'd just sorta made like tipping it to her when she had come to the door. I took it off but when I did it only confused her more. Then I forgave her ma and pa two more times.

I finally had to tell her who I was! When I did, her hand flew to her mouth and she let out a very audible gasp. That finished killing my pride. But I think what caused her not to be able to recognize me was that SHE had changed so much and also, maybe, needed her glasses changed. I know that was the reason. It couldn't have been anything else.

Of course, I know I had put on a little weight but not over 50 pounds, most of it all around the middle. And a little under the chin. Then, too, a little of my pretty curly hair, well, a right smart. ALL RIGHT, so I had got plumb baldheaded. But my eyes hadn't changed a bit. They were still about as brown as ever. And I still had my own teeth—all except three. One got knocked out by a swinging door back during MY WAR. Well, I don't care whether you believe it or not, but that is what my buddy told me when I began to sober, I mean WAKE, up. I got one put back in its place and I have been thinking some about having the other two put back in. But, I'd say, taking me altogether, that I hadn't changed hardly any. She sure had, though.

When she got over the shock of finding out who I was, she wanted to know all about me. She wanted to see pictures of my family and hear all about them. And I won't ever forget one comment she made. When I was showing her a picture of my grown son, she said, "My, My, he is a lot better looking than you used to be." Now how in the Sam Hill would you react to that sort of comment? I thanked her. That was all I knew to say. But I resolved, then and there, to take that boy's picture outta my wallet. That reminds me: I still have it there.

Poor ole Sally Kate never married. Maybe nobody else ever asked her but me. The moral of this story is: Avoid a meeting of this kind at all costs on account of there's been a lotta changes made in Old Sweethearts.

My writing about Alabama reminded me of something else, about how rich the soil was on our old farm. We never had to use any fertilizer. If we took extry good care of our corn, we would make a hundred bushels to the acre. If we took only middling good care of it, we would make seventy-five bushels. And if we didn't plant any a tall, we would still make fifty bushels to the acre.

It sure was hot down home too. I remember once in late June, me and Papa were gonna plant us some pop corn. He laid the rows off and then took our ole mule over to a shade tree to wait for me to drop the corn. I did. Well sir, just as I got it all dropped, it was so hot that the stuff started popping. In no time at all the ground was white, and that no good mule thought that it was snow and she laid down on the spot and froze to death. Yes, it used to get mighty hot down there. It was nothing at all unusual, up in the middle of the day, to look out and see every fence post on the place wilted to the ground.

THE CAP'N WAS MY BUDDY

Maybe they still call Marines who serve aboard ships Seagoing Bellhops. Whether they do or not I was one for about 30 months aboard the U.S.S. Texas. And, except for the first three or four months, I enjoyed this duty.

The reason those first months weren't as pleasant as the rest was mostly the fault of the Cap'n of the ship. I won't mention his name because I know some folks around here by the same name, and they're decent people.

This joker, for reasons known only to himself, didn't like Marines, and it seemed that he spent a lot of his time devising ways and means of making life miserable for us. And, you can believe me, the Captain of a battleship, if he puts his mind to it, can book up a foul routine for the crew.

When I got assigned as a Captain's Orderly, I seriously considered jumping ship. Captain's Orderlies had a chair outside the main door to his cabin. You sat there for four hours at a time, unless he sent you on an errand. This stinker wouldn't let us read, wouldn't let us do a darn thing but sit.

We heard he was leaving. There was jubilation, for sure, in the Marine compartment. We didn't know who'd replace him but, naturally, we felt that nobody could be worse and we hoped, whoever he was, that the change would be for the better.

It was! We got a long, lanky, 6 foot 5 incher. His name was R. R. M. Emmet. And it just so happened that I was his first Orderly after he came aboard. I was almost afraid to breathe, and I sure dreaded to hear his buzzer which would summon me inside his cabin for some errand.

It wasn't long in coming. I dashed inside and stood ramrod-straight in front of him as I saluted. He looked me up one side and down the other. Then he wanted to know my name. I told him, and he stuck his hand out and said, "I'm Cap'n Emmet." As if I didn't know!

Then he told me to be "at ease." And he wanted to know where I was from and lots of other things about me.

I couldn't help but think, almost from the beginning, that better days were ahead for the Marines on the Texas. Too, I gathered from his questions that he was in a way sizing us all up as he talked to me. I was doing my dead level best to give a good impression if that was, in fact, what he was up to.

After we'd gotten acquainted and he had told me how he wanted the job handled, it was almost a four-hour session, he told me that he wanted to take a nap and asked if I'd see that he wasn't disturbed.

Well sir, I want you to know that I'd not have allowed even the President of the United States to have bothered the "Ole Man."

Before he dismissed me, though, he said, "Now I know that every Marine on this ship is probably mighty anxious to know what kind of fellow you think I am. So, before your relief takes over, you tell the Corporal of the Guard to let him sit in on the bull session for a few minutes, then he can come on up here to his post."

So when I got back to the compartment every Marine in the detachment, including our Skipper, was in a big huddle waiting for my report. And you should have heard what all I told em! Every bit good!!

Why I could hardly wait to go back on my next watch.

And the next one was full of surprises too. As soon as I took over the watch I went in and sharpened all his pencils. After I'd gotten that done he asked if I could play Cribbage. I told him, "Yes, Sir, I can." And he called his house boy and told him to get out his cards and Cribbage board and set up the card table.

In no time at all there I was, a buck private in the Marines, playing Cribbage with the Captain of the ship. To begin with, nervous and scared were no names for what I was.

He knew it. He told me to take my cap, belt, and jacket off, and he said, "Now relax. If anybody comes to see the Captain they'll knock, we'll hear em and I'll invite em in." And he told me that he'd better not catch me playing to let him win. Said he'd personally throw me overboard if he did.

I sure hoped that no one would come in to see the Skipper while we were playing Cribbage. Only three did that first day: the Executive Officer of the ship, a full Commander, the Gunnery and Navigation Officers, both Lieutenant Commanders. I was afraid that one of them might order me shot at sunrise. You see, they stood at stiff attention as they addressed the Skipper. I just sat there mighty uncomfortable.

And that's the way things went for months. We'd play Cribbage, and when the Cap'n had snacks, I did too. He loaned me good books to read, and he always wanted to know what I thought about them. I had to give a book report on everyone of them.

When he'd go ashore, if we weren't tied up at a pier, he'd take all his orderlies ashore in his Cap'n's gig. We were sumpin Special. And there wasn't a Leatherneck aboard that ship who'd have hesitated to fight a room full of circle saws for Cap'n Emmet.

Well, you know the word spread mighty fast about my playing Cribbage with the Cap'n, and I took a powerful lot of fierce ribbing over it, but I know that there wasn't a man aboard, officers included, who wouldn't have swapped places with me ANY TIME.

When Captain Emmet came aboard the USS Texas, crew morale was at a mighty low ebb. We had had a tyrant before him, a little man in stature, as well as otherwise. He seemed always mad at everybody. Including God, we were pretty sure.

Maybe Cap'n Emmet knew all about this. Perhaps he was sent to relieve "Little Napoleon" to prevent a possible mutiny.

At any rate, the word got around real fast that this new Skipper was not only a big man physically but he was an officer, a GENTLEMAN, and a leader as well.

To have seen and experienced how this man operated, why honestly, you'd have thought he was always trying, with all his might, to sell himself. He was always wanting to know what we thought of him as if he had to "make it with us" to even keep his job instead of the other way around.

The next day after he assumed command the crew assembled for a "get acquainted session," he called it. It lasted about ten minutes and mostly it consisted of his informing us that he was new on the job and he was hoping that we would HELP HIM.

He told us where he was from, how many kids he had, how long he had been in the navy, and a few other things. Then he told us that he knew he could count on us to do our jobs, and in doing them we'd be getting HIS done. When he said, "That's all," there was the mightiest yell of "WELCOME ABOARD, SKIPPER," that anyone ever heard from about 1500 throats.

And, Mister, we meant it. In less than 24 hours that was a different ship. We had ten men in the brig at the time, but just minutes before the assembly we had gotten orders to turn them all loose. It was like Christmas, Thanksgiving, Easter, and the Fourth of July all rolled into one.

I think everybody felt sorta dazed. It just seemed unbelievable. Maybe we felt like the prisoners of war did when they were finally freed. He didn't say a word about doing away with discipline. I think he knew that we all understood that the regular rules and regulations still applied.

Every Saturday his stock rose higher and higher. For instance: When he inspected the Marine Detachment on topside, he said that we were all so shiny that he guessed he'd better have his dark glasses before he went any further.

And I'm here to tell you that the whole inspection stopped right there. He told his orderly to hold my rifle and he sent me for those sun glasses, and he told me where he "thought" they were. I beat it back to his cabin and got them, took back my rifle, and got in line. Then he proceeded to inspect the Marines.

On that first inspection he asked four men if they had heard from home lately, if they had a girl, if they had pictures in their wallets, and he wanted to see the pictures, right THEN! One of them told him that he didn't have a picture of his girl in his wallet but that he had a big one in his locker in the compartment. Cap'n Emmet said, "You show her to me when we get below." And, sure enough, when he got to this man's locker below decks, he said, "Now, let's see that young lady's picture."

Then, it was not at all unusual for him, when on inspection, to stop and comment on what a heckuva shoeshine a man had. And once he asked a buddy of mine if he thought he could put that kind of a shine and high gloss on HIS shoes. Naturally he answered, "YES, SIR," and danged if the Cap'n didn't send him right that minute to start the job on all of his black shoes.

Once when I was on Cap'n's Orderly watch and we had a big Cribbage game underway, the Navigation Officer came to see the Skipper about some navigation matter. We stopped the game, and the Cap'n lowered his head and looked at the officer over the top of his bi-focuses as he listened to the problem. Then this conversation ensued:

"Can't you see I'm busy?"

"Aren't you the Navigation Officer of this ship?"

"Yes, Sir."

"Then navigate, Young Man, navigate. Besides, I'm about to win this game here and you wouldn't want me to stop now, would you?"

With a grin about as broad as the beam of the Texas, the Navigation Officer said, "Absolutely not, Sir." Then he saluted very smartly, thanked the Skipper, did an about face, and took off.

After he was safely out of earshot, the Cap'n laughed the loudest you ever heard and said to me, "I'd betcha anything that that boy wouldn't feel a smidgen better right now than if he had just been presented the Congressional Medal. What do you think?"

And you can bet I certainly thought so too.

Needless to say, the Skipper was a CHARACTER, and morale and efficiency on the battlewagon went, and stayed, sky-high. It just seemed that the ship itself wore a broad happy smile!

My Buddy, the Cap'n? Man, he was EVERYBODY'S BUDDY.

MISCARRIAGE OF JUSTICE

I have an older sister whose name is Georgia Virginia. Why Mama ever named her that I have never been able to determine. Maybe Georgia because her hair was (some of it still is) almost the color of the red clay hills of Georgia. Virginia? Perhaps Mama had heard the song that contains this line, "Take me back to ole Virginny." Anyhow that is the name that Mama gave her.

And I learned pretty early that I could really get her dander up in a hurry by calling her a Georgey Jinny. Then there was another tried and true method of stirring her Irish fire, which always seemed to me to be close to the kindling point. That was by saying anything about her being red headed and freckle faced.

Virginia always said that she had "auburn hair with just a very few freckles."

Mentioning these items was just like lighting a short fused stick of dynamite. She did have a few freckles that she tried every known remedy for getting rid of, but they all failed. And all I had to do to get her wound up like a dime store alarm clock was say ANYTHING about em.

I was always very careful to never allude to either unless I had plenty of good running room and a long head start. One day she was out in the back yard at the pump. And I don't mean a Fairbanks-Morse but a pitcher pump with a handle. Anyhow she was busy cleaning some corn for dinner. She was always mighty good to help Mama which is a sight more than I could ever say for myself. I came around the house and thought I'd engage her in a little harmless conversation. I reckon I started out all wrong on account of I said, "You're a red-headed Jinny from Georgey." Anyhow she took spontaneous exception to my very opening remark.

She jumped up from there a-snorting fire and brimstone. I lit a shuck around the house on account of she had a big long butcher knife in her hand. I mentioned the color of her hair and those freckles one more time, when I was absolutely certain that I had a good safe lead. She hollered and said, "If I ketch you, I'll cut your head off, you little curly headed S.O.B." Only she didn't use those letters.

Well now, that there got through to me. It shocked me. The next time around I flew in the house and went to Mama as hard as I could fly and told her what that sassy youngan had called me. Mama dropped her sewing and called this little Georgey Jinny in the house to discuss the matter with her.

I could hardly wait for Mama to take Papa's razor strap to her back side.

Well, Mama began explaining to her what a terrible thing she had called her sweet little brother, and all about what those words meant. In no time a tall Virginia began squalling. She was as tender-hearted as she was high tempered. I kept waiting.

Finally Mama told me to go and get her a good switch. So, she was gonna beat her with a limb, cause that was what I brought her— one big enough to whip a mule.

Mama asked me if that was the switch that I wanted her to use. I assured her that it most certainly was. She said, "Well hand it here." As I handed it to Mama she grabbed a holt of me and all them thrashings she'd been promising me and saving up for me, I got em every one right then, plus a few more that I'd no doubt be due in the future. I'll tell you the truth, Mama flat tore me up and I's pretty sure she had misunderstood who had called whom what. She assured me that she understood perfectly.

When she got me tore up good and proper she told me that I was never to bother this sister of mine ANY MORE, and especially when she was working to fix us sumpin to eat.

Talk about a miscarriage of justice!!! This was it spelled with a capital T. I reckoned that if Virginia had cut my head plum off like she said she aimed to if she caught me Mama woulda called it justifiable homicide and let it go at that.

I don't get to see that sister very often, but there is one thing sure and certain, when we do get together it won't be but a few minutes before she asks me if I remember the time she was cleaning the corn etc., etc. I think I'll send her a copy of this tale so she can put it in a prominent place to remind her that, indeed, I DO REMEMBER the time!

ORDER IN THE COURT

Down home, in Andalusia, Alabama, when I was a boy, court week used to be the most entertaining single event of any season. At least it brought more people into town than nearly anything else. Of course there were always quite a few folks who had business that had to be transacted in court. Then there were a couple dozen or so jurymen, their families, defendants, plaintiffs, witnesses, and many, many more who just used this as an excuse to come to town.

A kind of carnival air seemed to prevail in town during court week. Mule trading usually picked up, and it wasn't at all unusual to see farmers bringing fat steers and pigs into town for sale during the week's festivities. The local merchants' businesses usually realized a sort of shot-in-the-arm effect from the stepped up activities.

An awful lot of cheese and crackers, sardines, Vienna sausage, potted meat, pork & beans, and Nehies were sold and consumed during court week. And there were many games of checkers and dominoes played, possum and coon hounds swapped, and an occasional crap game (galloping dominoes—dice) or poker game could be found if anybody was determined enough.

It's not quite like that anymore, either down home or around here. Folks have gotten mighty sophisticated these days.

But anyhow, court week was a big deal down home. I especially looked forward to it in the summertime cause that was just about the only thing sufficiently important enough to get me out of a lot of hoeing. Well, it didn't actually get me out of any, but it was an excuse to put it off a few days.

A real tragic disappointment for me back in those days was when it rained during court week. Although I could get out of hoeing if it rained, that didn't even begin to compensate me for missing out on all the gaiety in town.

Now you wouldn't think there'd be too much of interest going on to entertain a shirttail lad of twelve or thirteen and, sometimes, we did have to concoct our own diversion. However, I can't ever remember that this presented too much of a problem. Usually our difficulty was a lack of time to do all the things we had planned.

One of the most interesting amusements we ever had around the courthouse was shooting pigeons with our slingshots. You know how it is with pigeons and courthouses. I don't reckon it would hardly be a courthouse without pigeons. And it didn't make a bit of difference how many of them we managed to kill, there was generally an abundance of them for every court session.

A buddy and I were thinning em out pretty good one hot summer afternoon when, all of a sudden, we got grabbed by the nape of the neck and the seat of our britches and hauled into court as bona fide defendants. We had no idea why either until this big raw-boned deputy sheriff got us up there in front of the meanest looking judge I ever laid my eyes on. Tell you the truth, he was also the first judge I had ever seen. Well, with his being a great big fat man, plus his imposing looking black robes, and his glasses resting about half-way down his long nose, and him sweating and mad, I'll tell you, His Honor was just about the most awesome looking creature I could have ever imagined. But I'll guarantee you this much, there wasn't a doggone thing imaginary about His Honor. He was GEN-U-Wine, every pound of him!!

He took care of the interrogation himself. The first question he asked us was if we owned slingshots. Naturally now, being scared plumb purple, we told him, "Naw suh, Yo Honah." The fact that we both still had our slingshots clutched in our grimey hands sure didn't alter our testimony. That is, until he asked us whose we were holding. Then he explained something about the laws of perjury and the penalties thereof. We found out that perjury and lying are just a right smart alike.

Finally, after he had scared us slap outta several years growth, he got around to telling us with what we were charged. "You two boys," he said, "are charged with shooting me with a slingshot." And you never heard the like of guffawing as there was in that courtroom, and this brought on a lot of gavel whacking by His Honor and a mighty stern admonition of "Order in the court. Order in this here durn courtroom!"

When things kinda quietened down just a little, he warned everybody that if he so much as saw a smile on anybody's face he would hold them in contempt. This straightened everybody up pretty good.

Then he told us boys that since our crime was not covered in the statute books of the Sovereign State of Alabama he would have to confiscate our slingshots and ammunition. He directed the Clerk of the Court to take charge of that property and then he made us promise never to shoot any more pigeons around the courthouse while court was in session. We gave him our word on it.

According to Papa, who happened to be on the jury at the time, the old judge had just stood up to stretch when, mighty suddenly, he jumped and hollered. Papa said he must have swallowed his cud of Brown's Mule cause after he grabbed himself and hollered like a stuck hawg he had a terrible fit of coughing and got powerful red in the face.

It seemed that our aim must have been a little off and one of us had hit His Honor right in the, uh, well, smack dab on his DIGNITY. But like Papa said, he reckoned it was a good thing the rock hit him where he had a lot of padding and insulation instead of, maybe, hitting him in the head. Else we might have been charged with killing a judge.

I sure expected Papa to take a plow-line to me, or his razor strap anyhow, but he didn't. He said he guessed it was about the funniest thing that he had ever seen happen in a court of law. Course he did caution me some about shooting pigeons that happened to be sitting on a window sill of the courtroom.

MEDICARE'S TO COME
PETICARE IS HERE

If you think you lead a dog's life then you better read this for sure. And before you finish reading it I'll bet you decide that most dogs fare a sight better than you do.

First of all I want to tell you that I found out every bit of this startling information in a very reliable weekly news magazine. So you see, I have proof for what I am going to tell you. After all I'm not about to kid you ALL the time—just NEARLY all the time.

This entire article was about the expert medical care now being lavished on America's pets—dogs and cats mostly. In fact, even the title of the article was Peticare. Medicare may be a long way off but PETICARE is here.

One paragraph went something like this: In thousands of Veterinary Clinics and hospitals, pets are undergoing operations for cancerous tumors, cataracts, Caesarean births, hysterectomies, gall stones, and even heart and brain defects. Some aging dogs have been fitted with false teeth and contact lenses, and Jerry Lewis (comedian) supposedly spent $15,000 for his dog's hearing aid. A San Francisco veterinarian said, "Ninety per cent of the dogs in America probably get better medical treatment than half the people in the world."

This article said that some dog and cat clinics even boast blood banks and 24-hour emergency service complete with ambulances. The convalescing pets languish in air-conditioned kennels, munching special dietary foods while listening to piped in mood music.

And you think you lead a dog's life? Well, you might but I sure don't. For instance, I have been a patient in more hospitals than most

people have been in grocery stores. Not a single one that I was ever in was air-conditioned. Why, hardly any of them had this piped in mood music.

And as for munching on those special dietary foods—well, I'm sure all of you know how it is trying to get well on what PEOPLE hospitals feed you. That's why all your kinfolks and friends are all the time bringing fruit and candy and things like that when you are in the hospital. They are trying to keep you alive until you can get out and back home where you can get something to eat.

This enlightening article also pointed out that modern vets must also treat emotional problems. There was this one worried cat owner who reported his cat had turned nervous and sulky since the arrival of a new baby in the family—and I don't mean cat baby, but a people-baby. This vet was really on his toes. He psychoanalyzed this cat's trouble P.D.Q. as a case of sibling rivalry and advised the new father to lavish more attention on his cat, and prescribed tranquilizers for both of them.

One dog owner was so lonely for her pet that she called the clinic and asked the vet to bring her dog to the phone so she could hear him bark. The vet found his patient asleep but so as not to disappoint the owner or awaken his patient, he barked into the telephone while a happy owner cooed baby talk. Doesn't that touch you? I think this dog owner and the vet too were both a leetle tetched.

They said it wasn't anything unusual for dog owners to request a kennel with a view, send get well cards, and on special occasions to provide a Western Union boy to sing "Happy Birthday" to Fido.

It told about the prices. Modern day vets frequently charge $5.00 for an office call and $10.00 for a house call. And a typical combination of diagnosis, major surgery, and convalescence can cost as much as $2,000.00. One Atlanta mother of two (children, I think) moaned, "I owe more to my vet than I do to my family doctor."

Then also in Atlanta there is a Pet Heaven. A cemetery for cats and dogs. A few weeks ago a dozen shivering mourners stood around a casket containing the remains of INKY, an 18 year old Cocker Spaniel. A wreath had a rubber bone tied to it and the silk-ruffled casket contained the pair of shoes Inky loved to gnaw on.

But I don't guess people change much. I can remember years ago my sister and I had us a pet cemetery too. I also remember it was at a funeral we were having for one of Evelyn's old cats when we had one of our worst fights. The fight started when I told her, "That was the sorriest ole cat I ever conducted the funeral of."

We always had very nervous cats too. It would just tear em up emotionally for me to yell, "Sic em." This also affected Evelyn if she heard me yell that because she knew as well as those cats did that when I said "Sic em" that old Gyp (Gyp was my very valuable, well-trained sooner dog) would immediately put em up the nearest chinaberry tree or up a post into the scuppernong vine.

Why we even performed some limited surgery on our pets. When an old hog ripped Gyp's side open once, I sewed her up while Papa held her for me. The patient recovered but the hog died. That was the only hog killing I ever enjoyed.

(Epilogue: L. H. Conley of San Pablo, Calif., sent a note along with a Scout Straw Vote Ballot stating he was a Tar Heel by birth and a Democrat by choice, and made the following comment on "Cuz" Bagley's column concerning dogs. "There is a Dog-ologist (I suppose that is what you call them) near my home and I see people taking their poodles in to be groomed and bathed when I know they are on State aid. More power to his column." The letter was signed, "A dyed in the wool Johnson Man.")

WILLOW LEG

When one loses a friend I feel that he is diminished by an irreplaceable amount. At least, that is how I feel over the recent loss of one of my very best friends, Ammel Harding Baine.

I won't ever forget the first time I saw him. It was shortly after I'd gone back to work at Hiwassee Dam for TVA's Public Safety after WW II. One afternoon I happened to be standing near the front door of the old post office building in the village. I, along with several other people, was waiting for the daily mail delivery. A small battered flat bed truck pulled up in front and was loaded with pulp wood. The driver got out and walked, I thought somewhat awkwardly, up the steps to the building. He was dressed in an old G.I. shirt and trousers.

Before he got to the top of those steps it was obvious that he had an artificial leg. He stepped up to the window and Mrs. Clay Allen handed him his mail. Then he made his way back to that battered old truck, got in and, although the vehicle looked as if it might fall apart, it started immediately. And he headed on out with his load of pulp wood.

He wasn't out of sight before I went back inside and asked Mrs. Allen who that fellow was. She told me, and she also told me that he had been in the Army during the war and had lost that leg in North Africa. She also informed me that he was in the pulpwood business. Indeed, he was, and all by himself. That's right; he cut the stuff, loaded it, and did his own hauling.

I watched for him the next day and made it my business to meet him. In the course of our conversation I learned that because of his leg he hadn't been able to land a job up to then. He went on to tell me that he had a wife and baby to support and he couldn't do that on just what the government paid him for that leg. And he said, "Man, I've got to work at something and these hills are covered with pulp wood just waiting for somebody who isn't afraid of a little work."

A "little work"?! In my estimation there just isn't anything that could compare with that for HARD WORK. I wondered how on earth he could get up and down those hills, cut, load, and haul that stuff all by himself. I never learned HOW he was able to do it all alone. I just know that he did it.

I mentioned about his old truck starting immediately when he tried to crank it. Listen, that man could fix anything! And, although the body of that vehicle looked sorta beat up, the motor was in tip-top shape. He saw to that.

Shortly after our getting acquainted he did get a job with TVA as a filter plant operator. That's when he left the pulpwood business. A year or so later the filter plant job at Hiwassee Dam came open and he was transferred back home.

Besides his plant operating he had other things going on the side to take up his spare time and add to his income. He was an expert automobile seat cover builder. And he could and did fit those things on like they were molded to the seats. I had ordered a bunch of junk from some outfit once and they gave me a set of seat covers as a bonus. They said anyone could install them.

I spent an entire afternoon trying to install them. No soap. Finally, I took off for River Hill to get Harding to help me with em. He was busy at his big sewing machine. I told him my problem. He just quit where he was and in nothing flat he told me that the danged things wouldn't ever fit. I told him we'd just forget it. He said, "No, man, they just need a few altcrations."

He began ripping em apart and re-sewing em. In about an hour and a half I left there with a set of seat covers custom built. And installed.

In addition to his seat covering business he also reupholstered furniture. He could make it look as if it had just come from the factory. And on water pumps he was sumpin else. Mine made a habit of breaking down. I got ashamed of calling on him but was compelled to several times. Once he came and listened to it try to start. He said, "Take that motor out of there and set it up here. I believe that it's just got an ant or sumpin on the armature shorting it out.'' He took it apart and you know what? That was exactly it!

Not very long after getting to know him I thought that I would like to join the Masonic Order. I mentioned it to him. He encouraged me and brought me an application form. Somehow I was voted in. When I was initiated I learned that he was the Worshipful Master. He'd never even mentioned that to me before.

I'm sure that you have attended Masonic funerals and noticed that the Master always wears a hat. Same thing when he is presiding in the Lodge. But Harding never owned a hat, or, at least, I never saw one on his head except when he was serving as Master of the old Unaka Lodge of which we were both members. He'd always borrow somebody's hat after he got there. I always wore mine to lodge on account of my bald head. A time or two he borrowed my hat and with my being just a pinhead my little bitty hat just would sit on top of his head. But he still looked and acted mighty dignified while he was presiding.

After he'd borrowed my hat a time or two I just began putting it on his head as we'd go into the lodge.

He was the filter plant operator at Hiwassee Dam during the time the reversible pump turbine was being installed and in addition to those duties he also served as the maintenance man for the village. That meant that he kept the electrical and plumbing stuff going for the villagers.

There was one lady, our next door neighbor, who had some silly something she claimed needed fixing just about every day or two. Harding was always mighty courteous and helpful. He'd go tend to whatever it was. He confided to me, though, that she was a real nuisance and that her husband could've fixed every bit of it when he got off work, and in just a few minutes.

One day Mrs. Nuisance called him and began telling him her problems. When she hesitated to get her breath Harding said, ''Mam, I've just broken my leg.'' He had meant to go on and tell her that as soon as he got his wooden leg fixed he would be down to see about her difficulties. But Mrs. Nuisance didn't give him a chance to tell her anything else. She hung up and called Public Safety. I happened to be on duty and she was just screaming into the phone. I tried to calm her down. No deal. I told her that I'd go up and see about him.

I felt sure that he hadn't broken his good leg or he'd have called us. I took off up there and as soon as I walked into the plant, I called upstairs to him. I said, "Hey, Hardie, which leg did you break?" He laughed loud and long and assured me that he'd just broken a little something on his old wooden leg as he was going up the steps in the plant. Then I told him about the phone call from the lady. He said he figured that she'd gone berserk when he told her that he'd broken his leg.

He also told me that he'd tried to call her back and tell her but her line was busy so he just gave up. She was calling everybody in the village about his "accident."

After visiting a few minutes with him I drove on back and stopped by the lady's house and told her what had happened. Her only comment was, "My God, I didn't even know he had a wooden leg!" Harding told me later that she never called him again. He also said that if he'd known that her knowing would do so much good he'd have told her himself.

He had another problem while he was the filter plant operator there. A couple of families had dogs that'd bite. But he laughed and said that he'd broken them both from biting. I asked him how he'd done it. He laughed and said, "When I saw that they were determined to bite me I just stuck this old willow leg out at em and let em bite that." He said, "They both ran off yelping with their tails tucked between their legs!"

Oh, the many amusing stories I could tell about him would fill a book!

ELLIE-PYE

It happened a lotta years ago. None of your business HOW many.

We were in study hall at Dear Old Andalusia (Alabama) High School. It was a big, long room and had youngans in it from several grades. We were sitting near the back of the room. I was in the 8th and this saucy little ole skinny girl who was sitting just across the aisle from me was in the 7th. Our teacher was just about the size of said skinny youngan, soft spoken and mild mannered. In other words, she wasn't the kind who hollered at chillun. But she sure believed in keeping order and for some reason or other she thought that we should all STUDY! Her name was Miss Barrow.

That little bitty girl youngan I mentioned above wasn't making any kind of show at studying. Hadn't even cracked a book or nothin. And her hair! She had just had a permanent or sumpin and every hair on her head was standing straight up, straight out, and mighty frizzled up. But I hadn't even noticed that part or anything about her until I began hearing this whacking, smacking racket. It went on and on, and very rapidly.

When I really looked her over, I saw that she was leaning forward and filing her fingernails as she whacked merrily away on a wad of chewing gum. Now this gum chewing just wasn't allowed at Andalusia High. No sir! I tried my best to get my mind on my history book. No dice. Whack, smack, whack, whack! I sure hoped that Miss Barrow would ketch her and would tear her up. Only I knew that she was not the tearing up kinda teacher. Anyhow I hoped she'd ketch her.

It wasn't long until Teach spotted all that whick-whack-smacking. She instructed Ellie to come to her desk. I saw her point the waste basket out to Miss Ellie. That Ellie kindly strutted over to it and made a "spittoie" sound in in its general direction and then flounced back to her seat. Why, nobody ever saw a more smart alecky youngan! She leaned her head down and between whacks and more smacks she said to me, "If that silly teacher even THINKS I'm a gone spit my gum out she is KaRazy, Kay-razee!"

In a minute or so Miss Barrow came softly, very softly, back toward us and stopped beside Ellie. She said, in almost a whisper, "Give me that gum." Ellie did. But mighty reluctantly. On account of, you see, back then a piece of chewing gum was a rare treat. Hard to come by. What we did was, if we got a holt of some, we'd chew it all day, maybe for several days, and every once in a while we'd drop it into the sugar bowl so as to re-sweeten it up. And, at night we'd stick it up on the wall or on the bedpost. Sometimes we'd go to sleep with it still in our mouths. Yeah, and a lotta times wake up with it stuck in our hair.

It was several days later when I learned who that little snip of a smart-alecky girl youngan was. She was Ellie O'Neal . . . twin sister of my very own D. E. Only I sure didn't realize THEN that she would ever wind up as my own sister-in-law. No Siree!

D. E.? You never heard of that term? Well, familiarize yourself with it on account of you'll probably see it used many times in the future. It means Domestic Engineer. You know, for housewife.

No need for me to even try to tell you how mad Ellie was after Teach took her chewing gum. I couldn't even begin to describe that. No way. And I sure wouldn't put on paper some of the things Ellie said about Miss Barrow. Nobody would print them.

Now I never did actually get good and acquainted with Ellie until we'd both done some growing up, a right smart, and I got powerful interested in her twin sister.

Won't ever forget my taking Ellie and Nell to a picture show one night. Reason I took both of em was on account of I had to get Ellie to talk Nell into THEIR going to that show with me. It was a kind of a date like.

Along about here I'd better explain that there's a slight difference in these twins. If sumpin was funny Ellie believed in responding with a whopping belly laugh. And those were my own sentiments.

D. E. was very quiet, shy, and mighty reserved. She didn't like to have any kind of attention drawn her way. Ellie was zackly like me, she didn't care.

And that show that night was powerful funny. And me and that Ellie did do a sight of laughing way out loud. So did a lot of other folks. But Nellie, my future D. E., sure kept extry quiet. In fact, she was humiliated.

On our way home afterward Nell wouldn't even walk with us. No siree. She flounced way out in front and near bout took off in a trot. Now that sure made me mad, and Ellie too. I hoped that Ellie would scratch her good with her long fingernails—same ones she's had since I first met up with her in that study hall.

But I fixed that Nell! I sure did! When I got home I wrote her a note in red ink and took it and a big picture of her and went back to her house and put both of em behind the front screen door.

But back to Ellie.

Quite a few years later she and D. E. lived with Bob and Mary in Atlanta and they were working there. Mary is an older sister. Bob Miller was her husband and at that time he was SOME softball player. One night his team was playing a game so Ellie, Nell, and Mary went to see the game. Now, as I told you, Ellie usually made a lotta racket. Bob came to bat and on the first pitch he hit it over the fence for a long home run which scored two men in front of him and won the ball game. Ellie was yelling her head off along with a bunch of other folks who were happy about that home run. Just as Bob crossed home plate Ellie jumped up and screamed at the top of her lungs, "He's OUR husband!"

Now I could hardly wind this up without mentioning that this same Ellie since married and had a coupla mighty bright youngans. A boy named Billy and a girl, Michele. I'll brag a little on this Michele. She is some kinda beauty and I just know that she never, ever did look like her mama did in that study hall. She is both beautiful and brilliant. And she majored in French in college and wound up studying at the Sorbonne in Paris, which is about the same as saying that she was a Rhodes Scholar.

Ellie and Michele spent a few days with us last month and, tell you the truth, around somebody all that smart, as Michele is, I feel kindly ignorant. So, to sorta even things up I challenged her to take a little tricky aptitude test. She very readily agreed. The test consisted of twenty questions. If you got from 16-20 correct, you earned a rating of genius, 12 to 15—above normal, 8 to 11—normal, 4 to 7—subnormal, and below 4—idiot. Now a heap of mighty smart folks who've submitted to my aptitude test have wound up in the subnormal and idiot bracket. On account of it ain't nothing but trick questions. But this Michele got 19 out of the 20 questions.

I was flabbergasted, but then I remembered how smart a girl she was. And then I gave the test to that Ellie. She, too, wound up in the genius bracket. I decided that a heap of Michele had rubbed off on her mama over the years.

But you know what happened? Them Scamps! They'd both taken that same durn test somewhere BEFORE! Which just goes to prove that that Ellie sure ain't changed much from what she used to be. She still enjoys a real good belly laugh and she doesn't care one bit if it's at the expense of her very own brother-in-law. And a heap of Ellie rubbed off on Michele cause she can flat do a first class belly laugh herself and she did do one at her pore ole baldheaded uncle.

The only question she missed was done deliberately.

BOOT CAMP

From what I've read and heard Boot Camp in the United States Marine Corps has changed a lot since I was a recruit at Parris Island, South Carolina in 1937. Of course, some of those changes have been good, I'm sure, and I believe that some of them weren't so hot. Discipline may not be what it once was; maybe esprit de corps isn't exactly the same as it used to be.

However, the methods used to make Marines out of raw civilians back in those days were, to say the least, somewhat harsh. Anyhow, they were rough as a cob when yours truly was trying to make it through there and striving terribly hard to stay in one piece.

Having seen my Uncle Mac attired in his mighty glittering uniform inspired me to want to become one. I learned later, and much to my sorrow, that I should have consulted with him very extensively before I ever signed on the dotted line. I kinda feel that he would have said, "Listen, boy, this ain't the outfit for you. You go and see if you can enlist in the Salvation Army."

Maybe I would have listened to him. However, I imagine that I'd have gone on with it, if for no other reason than to prove to him that I was tough enough to take it.

A good friend of mine Pharon Cooke, nicknamed "Tarzan" because of his fine physique, and I decided that the Marines was for us. We filled out our papers and mailed them in the same day. We never knew why but they sent for me first and so I headed to Macon, Georgia for the physical and other exams. Unfortunately, I made it and they put me on a bus for Parris Island.

Not a soul spoke a harsh word to me until I set foot inside the gates of Boot Camp. That's when the harshness began and it didn't end until the night before my platoon was to ship out some four months later.

The afternoon of my arrival about 60 of us were herded together and marched to the barber shop. Several times I held up my hand with the intention of telling our D.I. (Drill Instructor) that I didn't need one on account of I had just had a brand new one the day before I left the warm hearth of home in Andalusia, Alabama. I learned later that it was just as well that he either didn't see my hand or just ignored it.

When we got to the Post Barber Shop our D.I. said, "All of you who need a haircut take one step to the front." About a dozen guys took that step. That was when he told us about going on into the shop when our names were called. He took out a roster and began calling names.

There were a couple of guys whose names began with "A" but both of them had taken a step indicating that they needed a haircut. He directed them to go on in on account of the haircut we were about to get would be a FREE one and we might as well get all that was coming to us for free.

Then he told the rest of us that as soon as the first man came out he would call the next name. My name being Bagley enabled me to get in that shop in a hurry. However, I had seen a couple of guys come out of there whose head hadn't exactly been clean shaven but they came mighty close. I thought that I'd sure not have my hair fixed any such way.

I sat down in the chair and that was the nicest barber. He said, very softly, almost as if he wanted to have me as a real buddy, "How would you like to have me cut your nice hair?" Then I explained about just having had a haircut a day or so ago and about my sideburns, and maybe just a little taken off the top.

My, oh my, I did have such pretty curly hair and it was the only characteristic that I had that I thought was really sumpin. Well, I did have a reasonably fair set of teeth too. But my hair!

After I'd done my explaining that cussed critter laid those clippers right against my skull, and right in the middle and he turned em on full speed ahead. Suddenly I felt plumb sick. He must have realized how I felt because he apologized and said that bit about having made a "slip o' th' clip" and all about how he hated it but during his brief apology he didn't slow those clippers down one bit. As he zapped off my beautiful curly locks he was busy telling me that he knew I'd want it all evened up.

I want you to know that before I could swallow more'n three times he had me cleaned off and I's on my way back out to rejoin my platoon. And a peeled onion just ain't no adequate word to describe how my head looked. I didn't even have as much left then as there is up there now.

The next place our sweet D.I. took us was to the supply room where we hurriedly changed from our civilian clothes, and I mean all the way to the skin. And then when we were all buck naked they started us down a line to get skivvies—underwear.

Now during this stripping down process a couple of the young lads vocally expressed a reluctance about undressing THAT completely in view of the fact that there were no window shades. I won't tell you what the D.I. told them before he closed with, "Now you're gonna find out how much a few fig leaves meant to Adam and Eve."

DRAWING BUCKETS

Boot Camp in the U.S. Marines back in 1937 was sumpin else, as I mentioned before.

After visiting the supply room and getting our clothing and turning in our civvies we headed for the PX—or Post Exchange—to draw our buckets. Now these were extry special buckets. They were all of the 10-quart galvanized variety and chock full of goodies. Lemmee see, they contained a scrubbing brush with very stiff bristles, for scrubbing our garments. Then there was a couple of big bars of G.I. soap. It sorta smelled a little like the old Octagon soap that used to come in a wrapper with a coupon on it, which if you were ever able to save enough of em up you could get some wonderful prizes.

Then we had some tooth paste and a brush and a bar of white looking soap which we found out later was our "toilet soap" but it didn't smell a bit better than our G.I. clothes washing soap.

Somewhere in that bucket was a big roll of heavy string which had two tiny brass rings, or clamps, set very close together about every six inches apart. We were instructed to cut this string between these two little brass things which made us have, maybe, about forty short pieces of string. Came to find out that these were to be used to tie our freshly scrubbed clothes to a big bunch of ropes that were attached to pulleys and all this suspended between a couple of tall poles. These ropes would be lowered so we could all reach them and tie on our clothes. Then the "pole men" would hoist all this up sky high to wave in the breezes and dry. Very practical!

Somewhere down about the bottom of the bucket we found something that was a pure insult to us all. None of us could determine any practical use for it a tall. It was a COMB! And, after our visit to our friendly barber who'd clipped our locks off a heap closer to our skulls than that man did Samson's in the Bible!

Among all that great stuff was a safety razor, a pack of blades, and actually some shaving soap which made just a wee bit more lather than our G.I. clothes washing soap. They had been thoughtful enough to include a shaving brush that we all thought was probably designed for the soldiers of the French Foreign Legion on account of the bristles of it were—well, I believe that we could have brushed horses down with and made em look might sleek.

They had also included a small mirror which was powerfully discouraging to look into after our haircuts. However, they did come in handy for shaving.

As for that shaving. Why, I had never shaved a lick in my life and neither had the most of those lads. All most of us had was a tiny bit of peach-like fuzz. But we were instructed, in the tenderest of terms, to have all that removed before we assembled for reveille the next morning.

I said I had never shaved any. Well, I had, too, tried it with Papa's straight razor a time or two and wound up just about to bleed to death about the face. I gave that up as a dangerous job. Until I suddenly found myself in the U.S. Marines. Sure was glad that they gave me a safety razor. That is, since they did insist on everybody's shaving every day.

My first night at Parris Island was a rough one. You see, I's so shook up after being talked to, I mean hollered at, by such motherly tender, loving drill instructors, I, along with many others, hardly slept any. So, at 5:00 a.m. the next mornig when some bugler blew reveille we were all pretty near worn out before the day even began.

At 5:30 we heard a shrill whistle blow and we tumbled out of the barracks and lined up for roll call.

Our D.I. was a huge hulk of a man. He had a belly on him that made him look as if he was about three years pregnant. His lower lip drooped a way down which gave him the appearance of having a permanent snarl on his face. He was about 13 feet tall and must've weight 900 pounds. And when he walked, well, he was slue footed and was just about the most un-military looking critter I'd ever seen.

Oh yeah, on account of that big fat lower lip he had we all called him "Liver Lip" Gordon. Gordon was his real name but I know he couldn't have been kin to anyone else by that name. In fact, I am pretty sure that he didn't have ANY human kinfolks. Tell you the truth, we all decided that he hadn't been born noways a tall like any human being. It was generally agreed that, instead, he'd just been blowed out of a seabag.

Anyhow, there we were all lined up in a double rank and we had already been told to answer, "Here, Sir," when we heard our names called. Liverlip began calling out names. He yelled, "Bagget," and immediately two guys answered, "Here, Sir" . . . the boot whose name was sure enough Bagget and I.

Liverlip all but exploded and before it was over I sure wished that he had on account of we were all about to freeze to death and maybe some of the heat from the explosion would have warmed us a little. Besides that we were all scared stiff.

But here came Ole Liverlip down the line with his flashlight and his roster. He screamed, "Where's Bagget?" Bagget held up his hand and so did I on account of, you see, I thought this monster was mispronouncing MY name. He asked Bagget how he spelled his name. He told him.

Then he asked me the same question. Naturally I spelled mine for him. That was when he said a mighty lot of VERY harsh things to me as he reached through to the rear rank and grabbed me by the front of my fatigue jacket. He dragged me through there and was shaking my teeth out as he slammed me all over that ground. All the time this was going on he was impressing on me how to spell my own name.

When he got tired of wearing the ground out with me he slammed me back toward my place in line and knocked over two or three Boots in the process.

But, you know what, after that little incident I didn't have a bit of trouble waiting until MY VERY OWN NAME WAS CALLED—which was Bag-lay according to ole Liverlip. That's right. And we all had to stand out there in that frigid, tooth-chattering wind and cold while I spelled it at the top of my voice for about five more minutes.

I always did wonder if that humongous monster ever did learn that my name was spelled Bagl-E-y.

SEMPER FIDELIS

For those of you who don't already know, Semper Fidelis, in Latin, means ALWAYS FAITHFUL. That is the motto of the United States Marines.

I won't ever forget what a lot of us boys said after we got to Boot Camp in regard to that Latin phrase. Our pay as privates was $21.00 a month, and after they took out 20 cents each month for hospitalization, that left us a mighty lot of money to enjoy ourselves with. A few of those jokers were smart enough to get a powerful heap of jollies out of their $20.80.

Anyhow what we said was, "I thought that Semper Fidelis meant $75.00." Of course, we knew better than that. Well, some of them did anyway.

Right after getting out of high school, I was lucky and got me a job with the WPA making about $5 or $6 a week. Pharon Cooke—nicknamed Tarzan and who enlisted in the Marines at the same time that I did—did better than I. He landed a job with a dry cleaner driving a pickup and delivery truck. In no time at all he got a big raise and was put to work in the shop pressing clothes and mending some of them at the get-rich-quick pay of $9.00 a week. And he had a promise of 10 bucks per week if business stayed good.

Well, Tarzan and I got together often and discussed our mutual prospects of becoming rich men eventually at the rates we were going. Actually, what we did was to talk about the fact that we weren't getting ANY place. I'd just come back from Pensacola, Florida and, having seen my Uncle Mac in that gloriously beautiful, dress blue uniform of his with that red stripe down his leg, I told Tarzan all about that. I began working on him and finally persuaded him that we ought to join the U.S. Marines. Yeah, that's what I did. Convinced him too! And in the process talked him into giving up a good, soft, easy job of $36.00 a month for one that didn't pay any $75.00 a month, as we'd said we thought that Semper Fidelis meant, and taking one that paid only $21.00. I'll tell you this much, if I'd had half a chance after I first hit that Island, I mean on that very first day when I began seeing how things were gonna be, I'd have called him, wired him or SUMPIN and told him, "Whatever you do, don't take that trip to Macon, Georgia and join nothing like this outfit."

I mentioned that we talked of not getting any place in the jobs we had. That was right; we certainly weren't. So, what did we do? We joined the Marines so we could get no place faster.

On top of the bad pay situation we didn't get put into the same platoon. I came in with a group that filled the ranks of Platoon No. 4 and Tarzan got there three or four days later and wound up in Platoon No. 5. We didn't get to even see one another but, I think, three times while we were in Boot Camp.

After Boot Camp he went to Quantico, Virginia to an aviation outfit. I went to Sea School and thought I was flat headed for the Naval Academy. I didn't make it. However, I did pass the entrance examination which, at the time, I thought was sumpin else. I was gonna get myself a jam up college education, all at government expense. And besides that, I'd come out as an Ensign in the Navy or a Second Lieutenant in the Marines.

Tarzan Cooke worked on planes a while there at Quantico and was selected to go to Pensacola to Naval Flight School. At that time a few enlisted men got to attend that, and they came out as Flying Sergeants. When WW II came along, the Marines commissioned all their flying sergeants. Then there was my buddy Tarzan a big second john. And I????

Let me tell you about that. After studying my head off for months while aboard the USS Texas and missing out on a mighty lot of good liberties (shore leave), I was allowed to take the entrance exam for the Academy and passed it. Passed it good. In fact, four out of the five aboard who were working toward that goal passed the exam. We were a mighty happy bunch of youngsters.

Then the axe began to fall. Clayton F. Crunk from New York got real unlucky and caught a disease. One that flat knocked him out on account of the kind of disease it was. William F. Sammons from

Kentucky failed to make a bus connection from his hometown which made him AWOL for nearly 24 hours, and he got a Deck Court Martial, thus eliminating him. Ed Engle couldn't wait to get married, and he also couldn't keep the secret so that let him out, besides his flunking the exam.

Then it was my turn.

We were at sea. The Captain's orderly came to our compartment and told me that Cap'n Emmet wanted to see me. Now when the Captain of a battleship sends for an enlisted man, you could count on its being real good news or powerful bad.

It was powerful bad. For me. I went in after reporting "as ordered." As soon as I walked in, Cap'n Emmet told me to have a seat. The look on his face was one of foreboding. I thought I could tell that he had something to tell me that wasn't going to be good.

There were honest-to-goodness tears running down his cheeks, and he said, "Bagley, I don't believe I ever hated to tell a man anything as much as I hate to tell you this." My heart simply seemed to hit the steel deck beneath my feet. I was sure that he was going to tell me that Mama had died, although it wasn't customary for the Captain to pass out this kind of news. That was usually the Chaplain's province.

Cap'n Emmet then went on to say, "Son, you're not going to get to go to the Naval Academy because as this radiogram says here, you'll be 20 days beyond the maximum age limit by the time the plebe class begins."

Well, I couldn't possibly describe the terrible disappointment I had. Cap'n Emmet must have known exactly how I felt because he told me to just sit where I was as long as I felt like it. He also saw the tears in my own eyes. He told me that he knew just how much I had been looking forward to it. Told me that he'd been looking forward to all our getting to go and then he added, "Now, only one of you five will make it." I was still so shocked and disappointed and heartsick that I hadn't even managed a "Yes, Sir," or a "Thank you, sir." My mouth was so dry. And suddenly I had such a vicious headache. I sat there.

Cap'n Emmet, bless his heart, couldn't have acted any more disappointed and broken hearted had I been his own son. We both sat there for what seemed an eternity. He said a lot of things in an effort to comfort me, and among them were things about the United States Navy being too particular about some things.

I couldn't think of anything to say. Finally he untangled his long lean legs and came over and put his boney arm around me and patted me on the shoulders and he called for his cabin boy, a young Filipino, and he told him to bring us two strong Bourbons.

In a minute or two the young man brought them to us. Cap'n Emmet said, "Here, drink this. Maybe it'll make you feel a little better." I drank it down like a dose of medicine.

In a minute or so more the Cap'n said, "Now, son, you go on back to your compartment because you know all your buddies are wondering why I sent for you. And don't you do anything foolish now."

Somehow I made it back to the compartment, and I dreaded to have to relay such information to my buddies. Before I made it back to our compartment Cap'n Emmet had called our skipper, Marine Captain William B. McKean, and told him. I just know that when I got back to the compartment, Cap'n McKean had all Marines in the compartment, except those on post, and he told them what happened.

Now for a brighter note. The fifth man, A. J. Cronin from Boston made it on to the Academy. WWII began and they shortened the four-year course to three years. If they had waived that 20 days on me, maybe.... Well anyhow I'd have graduated within the proper age bracket. But Cronin made it and became a submarine officer. About a year or so after the war was over, my old shipmate had his picture on the cover of Life Magazine! He was the commanding officer of a group of our subs that was responsible for sinking a record number of Japanese ships in the Pacific.... Talk about proud! I was of him. And I couldn't help but remember the many times we'd studied together and how he always had difficulties with math—the calculus, trigonometry, any kind of math. And I was able to help him with it. My toughest area was in English and Ancient History. Cronin came to my rescue in those. So, who knows, maybe my helping him with his math contributed in a small way to our winning that war!

Oh no, I'm not forgetting the atom bomb and all the rest.

THE GLOVE SLAP

My, my! I slap forgot to mention that there was another item in that bucket we got at the PX. It was a small khaki-colored cloth packet. Liverlip Gordon told us that it was our "housewife." But I can assure you there wasn't anything inspiring in any manner about our newly acquired "housewives." The thing contained needles, thread, and a few buttons. You see, all this was taking place before the zipper age.

Why, I'd never sewn a button on or anything in all my borned days. However, I soon learned that little trick. Ole Liverlip had a mighty persuasive way about him which encouraged all of us to learn real fast.

Those fabulous buckets that we very early learned to prize so dearly, and its contents, cost us exactly $1.25.

Immediately after breakfast on my second full day at Parris Island we were all sorta herded to the dispensary for our physical exams. Now every man in that platoon had already had an exam at the places where we'd enlisted. In my case, Macon, Georgia.

Now in Macon I was practically frothing at the mouth on account of being so eager to pass that examination. Tell you what, even before I got to Macon I'd gone to our local dentist in Andalusia to have him check my teeth real good so's if there were any cavities he could fill them and the Marines couldn't use a cavity or two to turn me down on.

If I had known in Andalusia what I later learned at Parris Island I believe that I would have had my dentist drill me out a big hole in each tooth. On second thought, maybe I'd a just had him pull every tooth in my head.

Soon as we got into this great big room at the dispensary, a medical sailor—they called them Corpsmen—came in and told us to strip and line up around the four walls of the room. Then he took a bottle of mercurochrome with a cotton swab and he put a number on each of our left shoulders.

It was cold weather and there was heat in the room and all the windows were closed. I told you that all this was before the days of zippers. It was also before the days of any kind of deodorants, except MUM. Yep, there sure used to be one by that name, a white kind of salve stuff in a small jar. Sure enough I'd used a little under each arm but the big majority of those fellers hadn't. In just a few minutes the odor from 64 stripped naked fellers. . . . It was sumpin else and I wasn't sure I'd be able to stand it. Unfortunately I did. But by the time a doctor came in there with a mask on I could sure understand why he had it on. I'd betcha anything he had it saturated with some sweet smelling cologne.

It didn't take that doctor but just the fewest minutes to look in all our eyes, noses, and ears. Then he had us do a little exercise by instructing us to turn our backs to him, bend over, and grab our ankles. You see he wanted us to turn our backs on account of he knew that might just be a little embarrassing to us. He sure was a mighty considerate gentleman.

After he'd satisfied himself with our posture—well, what else could he possibly have been checking?—then he had us turn back with our right shoulders next to the wall. That's when a couple of these corpsmen started around giving us shots of I don't know what all. I won't ever forget that three of the guys passed out colder'n a mackerel. Actually I don't think they passed out from the shots. I think the odor in that room is what got to them.

Next place we went was to the dental office. That didn't take but just a very few minutes.

Then we were back outside and all lined up with our ever-loving Liverlip. He escorted us back to the barracks and told us to get ready for chow.

After chow we made a trip to the armory where we drew rifles, bayonets, cartridge belts, and packs. Then we headed back to the barracks again and were given just enough time to ALMOST make it back to our bunks where we left bayonet, scabbards, and packs. The whistle blew again and we practically flew back to get in ranks with our guns and bayonets.

The first thing Liverlip told us was that those weapons were NOT G-U-N-S, they were our rifles, or pieces. And he impressed on us that we were to take care of those things regardless of whatever happened to us. Said they'd be our best friends. "Why," he said, "before you get out of here some of you will be even sleeping with em." He was right. No telling how many of those guys actually had to sleep with their rifles, I mean PIECES, in their beds, under the kivvers with em. That was just a sort of mild punishment for some little infraction of Liverlip's rule and regulations.

Each of those "pieces" and the bayonets were covered up with cosmoline. That's a dark brown greasy mess that was used to prevent rust. We were each given some kind of solvent and instructed on how to disassemble those pieces and get all that gunk off and out of same. Now he didn't mean "nearly all" out and off. He meant every smidgen OFF and OUT.

Of course there were a few of the men who didn't quite manage to remove absolutely ALL of it. On inspection when any of it was found, our beloved D.I. always knew how to get the remainder out and this he would deposit on our faces, with the explanation that he was sure we would be able to remove it easily from there.

He directed us to just let it stay on our faces until after supper when we took our daily baths.

In addition to Liverlip we had two other D.I.'s by the names of Corporals Peck and Sharit. They were Liverlip's assistants and what he couldn't dream up for us to do, Peck and Sharit did. I mean terrible and awful stuff.

One of Peck's favorite tricks was to have us put our buckets over our heads and shout our names, or some obscenity, to the tops of our voices. He'd have us march away from him and as we got farther and farther away, he would yell that he couldn't hear us and he would yell, "Louder, louder." A little of this would just about burst our ear drums. However, that little gimmick would certainly impress the point he wanted to make very indelibly on our minds.

After about 10 days under the tender care of our D.I.'s, we heard that we would get a new Chief D.I. We were all so excited. All were certain that whoever he was he'd have to be an improvement over Liverlip. We were just positive that the new man would most certainly help to relieve us of the many harsh treatments being accorded us by Peck and Sharit.

The whistle blew one afternoon right after we'd gotten back from chow. We all rushed out and when we lined up we saw a brand new face, a new sergeant, standing there where Liverlip had usually stood. He wasn't nearly as big as Ole Liverlip. He didn't look nearly as mean. In fact he sorta had a pleasant look on his face, and we all silently sighed in relief.

Then he began talking to us.

That was great. We'd already grown accustomed to being shouted at at every breath. Only trouble was that Sgt. Watson talked where he could barely be heard. But that was just ALL RIGHT with us. He was a soft-spoken man. Our nerves were really ready for some soft voices.

It was in February and the wind coming off that ocean was cold as ice. We noticed Sgt. Watson carried a pair of leather gloves in his right hand. Naturally we figured he's tough despite his soft-spoken words and would put his gloves on later. He didn't. Just carried em in his hand.

He had us open ranks and he proceeded to give us an inspection. He started down the line and before he got to me I just couldn't resist the temptation to cut my eyes toward him, just to get a tiny glimpse of him before he got right in front of me.

This proved to be a mistake. Certainly I knew that when a Marine is standing at attention he is supposed to keep his eyes straight ahead. And he ain't supposed to move them or ANYTHING. That was when I found out, along with several others, what Sgt. Watson used his gloves for.

When he stepped in front of me, he said, almost in a whisper, "You g3 + $%* + $?&, don't you ever take your eyes off STRAIGHT AHEAD again as long as you're in this outfit!" And as he finished whispering to me, he whacked me across the left side of my face with those leather gloves.

I was sure that half my face was gone, my left ear, and my nose. I felt certain that in just a few seconds I'd feel my own blood drenching me to the skin. I's sure that I'd never ever be able to smell again, hear out of my left ear, or even eat a bite cause I's just positive I's permanently disfigured.

Anyhow, that was how and when we all learned why he carried those gloves with him.

PLANS FOR A SLAYING

I always treated my recruits just exactly like I would have liked to have been treated when I was a Boot-recruit. That's a big lie, and I'm sure that you realized it if you've read any of the other stories I've written on the subject. Actually I began with this idea in mind: Of treating them kindly, etc.,; however, before I got through the first day of being a D.I. one Sergeant Milner changed my mind for me. He told me that it just wouldn't work.

A few days after that, Col. Louis R. Jones called all us new D.I.'s into his office and made it a lot plainer to us about how gentle and thoughtful we were to be toward our recruits. Said, "If I find a man who likes his drill instructor, I'll bust and transfer that D.I.!"

With Sgt.Milner's and the Colonel's admonitions in mind, I proceeded to be a mean buzzard. Actually that isn't exactly what my recruits called me. The "mean" part was right but not the rest of it.

One night after supper I walked out of my barracks and by the end of the two rows of tents that my platoon occupied. There were four men assigned to each tent but what I heard sounded like at least a dozen men. I was on my way to see a flick—movie to those of you who are uninformed.

When I heard my name being discussed, I stopped to listen. I shouldn't have because they were sure saying some mighty ugly things about Mrs. Bagley's No. 1 son. I was already aware that they did not hold me in very high esteem. Truth of the matter is that they just hated my guts. As I stood there and listened to them, I thought that if Col. Jones could have heard those boys he might have even promoted me on account of he would have been absolutely sure that

I was doing my job. At least I's doing it in such a way that none of them liked me even a little bit. Oh, he would have been so *proud*!

I don't have any idea what all I had done to or with them that day but whatever it was, it was sufficient to angry em up sumpin fierce. They were discussing how to KILL THAT LITTLE SHRIVELED UP (You can guess what!).

Now, since they were unquestionably discussing yours truly, and the plans they were trying to hash out, I found the listening extremely interesting. From the sound of the discussion they were having difficulties with several very important points. One was that they were not sure of the plan they would use. Three or four of them said it should be done with a bayonet or bayonets. They said this would be the quietest way. The suggestion was made that I should be shot. The shooting deal was evidently frowned upon on account of all the racket that'd make. However, one man said that he had managed to bring back a few rounds of ammo from the rifle range. This was definitely a No No.

A lad in the group mentioned that strangling me to death would be the quietest; there would be no blood, and they could manage that without leaving fingerprints, and a host of other things.

Sometime during this highly informative discussion, one of the very brightest of the lads mentioned that it just would not do for them to leave my body where it would EVER be found. He said that the killing would be pinned on their platoon. They were very much in doubt if they could swing the deal at all if my body was ever seen again.

For a few minutes they concentrated on how best to dispose of the body once they had done me in. They were about to decide that the earthly remains had to somehow be dumped into the big river which emptied into the ocean very near there. They were sure that sharks would enjoy a feast. Some of them were in a degree of doubt about whether a shark would even stick a tooth into the likes of me.

I had walked out of my barracks in plenty of time to go by the PX for some pogey bait before the flick began, but when I thought to look at my watch I realized that there'd be no PXing for me that night. I had already wasted a good bit of time and unless I wanted to miss that night's show altogether, I'd better get busy.

Without further ado I stepped to the flap of that tent and jerked it open and stepped inside. I believe that all eleven men saw me at the same instant. It seemed that they all yelled "TEN HUT" (Attention) as if they were just one man and as they did so they were all on their feet standing ramrod-straight and stiff.

For a few seconds I just stood there and didn't utter a word. Then, "Men, since I have been standing in front of this tent and hearing all your elaborate plans and since I was the subject of your important discussion, thought I would just step inside and have you continue." I ordered them to just go ahead with their plans. Told them just to relax, and take up where they left off.

Why, you could have heard an eyelash hit the floor. Nobody said a word. I don't believe a soul even batted an eye. I waited another few seconds. Then I roared at em. I spoke to them individually. Asked them if something had happened to their tongues. They each told me, "No, Sir." To make sure I had each of them stick their tongues out.

I had all eleven of em standing there with their tongues sticking straight out. One man stuck his out and immediately pulled it back in. I bellered at him and asked him who had told him to put it back in his mouth. He assured me that no one had but he "thought you just meant for us to let you see our tongues."

After bragging on em with a few choice compliments about what pretty tongues I thought they had, I told em to get their tongues back inside their faces. Eleven tongues disappeared. Then I invited them, one by one, to step to the door of the tent and show me how far they could spit.

Would you believe that not a single solitary one of em was able to spit? PERIOD! Pore devils. I knew just how they felt. I knew just how much they all really wished that they could ram a bayonet through me, maybe about 10,000 times.

Over and over I encouraged them to go on with their plans. Not a word was heard. Then I said to them, "Now I heard one of you (and I named him) admit that he had managed to bring a few rounds of ammo back from the rifle range. You come with me to your tent and let's get that right now." That man followed me out and went to his tent, and I relieved him of five rounds of .30 caliber ammo that he had hidden in the bottom of his foot locker. I had him dump all the contents of his locker on the floor of his tent. Then the two of us went back to the starting point.

I told them that I was going to the movies and that when I got back each of the 11 men must have me a set of beads consisting of 500 cigarette butts. I also told them that I'd hold an audit on each set of beads to be sure that there were the required 500 butts in each one.

Sure, I missed a little bit of the front part of that flick, but I really wasn't much interested in it anyhow.

When I returned, I called on my 11 would-be slayers and they had my beads ready. As soon as I was out of sight they had gotten the entire platoon out and had em all helping to light up, take one short puff, and then pass em to the bead makers to put on the strings. I heard the next morning that they had even managed to get a good bit of help from some of the nearby platoons.

Oh yes, after the bead audit that night, I had a very thorough inspection of everything those boys owned. I didn't find any live ammo or even any brass (spent rounds—hulls). Of course, I knew that I wouldn't; if any of them had had any, I was certain that they would have gotten rid of that while I was at the flick.

PARRIS ISLAND RABBITS

If you or any of your relatives ever went through recruit training (Boot Camp) at Parris Island, South Carolina, I certainly hope that you or they got treated to at least one rabbit hunt while there. It just so happens that I didn't get to go on one during my Boot Camp. In fact, I didn't even hear of such a thing until I went back as a D.I. However, soon after my returning I heard some fabulous tales about the sport, and that's exactly what I thought those stories were—just tales, and real wild ones at that.

The way the subject came up was when one D.I. remarked that his platoon had really been on the ball. They were sharp. So sharp that he said that he guessed he'd have to reward them with a rabbit hunt. That statement aroused my immediate interest, but so as not to appear overly ignorant, I kept quiet and learned from the discussion that followed just what this rabbit hunting deal was all about.

After listening to all the details I decided that I'd have to find some excuse to take my own platoon on a hunt. It wasn't long until my men had sharpened up to the extent that I felt it was time to do some rewarding of my own. Besides, I hadn't ever been on one, and I sure wanted to see how it worked.

I didn't let on to the recruits that I, too, was a novice in this rabbit hunting method. As far as they were concerned I knew all the answers.

One Saturday afternoon I informed them that we'd go on this big safari the next afternoon. Also told them that we would need a reasonable amount of beer which they would have to chip in and buy. In nothing flat there was more than enough in a couple of campaign hats to buy several cases. My assistant, Mickey McGuire, and I drove to Beaufort, South Carolina and bought the beer.

When we got back with our beer, we had to persuade a mighty ornery mess sergeant to allow us to stash it in his cooler until we were ready for it. I said "persuade," but what it actually amounted to was bribery. To begin with he insisted on a whole case but Mickey and I finally talked him into just half a case. 12 bottles.

After that was settled the old boy volunteered to bake us some bread and even allowed us to use his kitchen utensils to cook our rabbits—if we would invite him to the supper. Not only did we invite him but also his cooks.

Everything was all set to go. I's all excited about the deal and you can believe that our recruits were as well. I was excited about the prospects and also a little bit nervous because I'd never been on such a rabbit hunt, and I wasn't at all sure that we'd get enough rabbits. Might not even get ANY, I thought. But from all the discussion I had listened to, I was worrying needlessly.

Finally Sunday afternoon, right after the noon meal, I had the men fall out with rifles and bayonets. After they had gotten into formation, I told them that this was not compulsory and that if any of em wanted to stay in the barracks and write letters or whatever they were at liberty to stay behind. About six or eight stayed behind.

We had about a mile and a half to march out to the happy rabbit hunting grounds which were near the post farm. When we got into the woods and broom sedge a little ways, I had the men stack their rifles.

Up until the time I had them stack rifles, they were all assuming that we'd hunt those rabbits with Springfield rifles. Although they hadn't seen the first live round of ammunition, they were telling me later that they had decided that someone would bring the ammo to us. None of them said anything to me to the effect that they quickly came to the conclusion that I had flipped my lid, snapped my wires, and just gone plain nuts when I had em stack rifles.

Next I had em take their bayonets and cut sticks about three or four feet long. This was when they were positive that I was off my rocker. It wasn't the first time they'd thought about that. But they cut the cudgels and then I had them spread out in a big semi-circle and start walking through the broom sedge and yelling and bellering to the tops of their voices. I assured em that this would scare the bunnies out and when that happened they were to conk em on the head or any place they could whack em.

All of em looked at me as if my bread wasn't quite done, but they did exactly as I'd explained. My assistant, Mickey McGuire, told me that he was "some kind" of sure that I'd lost all my marbles. I wasn't absolutely sure that he's wrong either.

However, the big drive and hollering got under way and in a minute or two a cottontail jumped up and when he did you should've heard the war whooping. All that racket must've un-nerved the rabbit and before he'd gone but a few feet one of the boys clobbered him. That lad held that rabbit up and yelled something; this was language not printable! Anyhow, he couldn't have been any prouder if he'd been a big game hunter who'd just bagged a prize and trophy winning beast.

Getting that first bunny ignited some genuine enthusiasm and that bunch of lads went bananas. Then came the second, the third, and on and on.

After we'd bagged about 15 or 20, Mickey decided that he'd have to join in, so he borrowed a bayonet and cut his own cudgel. Soon he'd conked one on the head, and I just never, in all my borned days, ever saw anybody so tickled.

When we finally quit every man in the platoon had one rabbit slung from his cartridge belt and some of em had two. All together we had 60 or more of em and that was absolutely the happiest bunch of guys anybody ever saw.

We were marching back right down the main road of the Island, and I allowed them to talk and laugh or whatever, just told them to stay in step and in formation. Told em that there's no telling who might come driving along.

The second car along was a big black Essex with a two-star flag on it. That was nobody but the Commanding General of the Base, Major General J. C. Breckinridge! My heart flew past my mouth to the top of my head. I hoped that the ole boy would just drive right on by us and not see the first rabbit.

I called my men to attention and we rendered a salute as he passed. He must've been driving about 10 or 12 miles an hour and he SAW. He stopped his car and backed up. I just knew I's in for it. Maybe there was a rule or regulation or order—or sumpin—against hunting rabbits.

He wanted to know my name first of all, and then he wanted to know all about the hunt. I explained it all to him. He expressed amazement and then he told me that when I got ready to go on another hunt to let him know because, as he said, he wanted to see that happen. I assured him that I'd certainly let him know. After he'd left us, I wished that I had told him that ANYTIME he wanted to go, all he'd have to do would be to let me know and I'd be glad to drop any or EVERYTHING and take him.

I sent word twice, but he couldn't make it right then, so I's told by his orderly.

When we got back to our barracks, the recruits cleaned those rabbits and we had a big cook out. And that was the happiest bunch of lads!

After the General left us that afternoon, one of the lads who was marching right beside me said, "Sir, that was the most fun I ever had in my life with my britches on."

Don't go jumping to any wrong conclusions. What he meant was that he'd had more fun when he was back home on the farm and "going in a washing" in the old swimming hole wearing nothing but his birthday suit.

MEET JOHN GLOWA

The reason recruit training in the U.S. Marines was called Boot Camp was on account of it wasn't anything unusual to have a D.I.'s boot, or shoe, planted mighty sharply on one's posterior.

Anyhow, our training got seriously underway immediately. In fact it really began as soon as our feet touched the ground at Parris Island, South Carolina.

Among the first things they did was to line us up according to height. My being a runt placed me at almost the end of the line. Already I'd wished many a time that I hadn't quite met that minimum height which was 5 ft. 6. I just made it under the wire with a whopping 5 ft. 6 and one-fourth inches. I weighed in at exactly 119 pounds and I learned later that 118 pounds was the minimum weight. You see, if I hadn't been such a glutton and turned into such a big glob of blubber, I'd never have had to undergo all that painful torture that I did in boot camp. I'd not even have been there!

They divided us into eight man squads and I wound up as the assistant squad leader in the runt squad. Yeah, that's what they called us. During the course of this putting us into squads one of the D.I.'s asked if any of us had had any previous military training. I made the mistake of raising my hand. However, I thought I might as well because it was all over my enlistment papers that I had been in the C.M.T.C., and the Alabama National Guard.

My having had this previous training only resulted in my getting watched a heap closer than a lot of the other "Boots" who, if they'd had any, didn't admit it. I only made assistant squad leader because of my altitude, elevation, or height. The guy who wound up as our squad leader was a jerk by the name of John Glowa from

Pottstown, Pa. And I want to tell you that he didn't know his right from his left foot and kept the entire runt squad in hot water just about all the time.

I don't believe that his being from Pennsylvania had a thing to to do with the trouble he kept us in. I sure hope not on account of I'd always had a lot of respect for that state with just two exceptions: 1. John Glowa and 2. They got on the wrong side during the Civil War which made all its natives damyankees.

Now, those guns, I mean pieces or rifles, I mentioned earlier, weighed exactly 8.69 pounds. That doesn't sound like much, does it? Of course not! However, that later turned out to be an enormous weight.

For the first few days they had us leave our pieces in the barracks and a mighty determined effort was employed to teach us to march. This was called close order drill. Now, I already knew all about that because of my experience in C.M.T.C. and the National Guard. But I can tell you this much: When some bum in front of you or behind you gets out of step then you're either stepping on his heels or he's doing it to you. So, my knowing how to march wasn't a great deal of help.

Oh yes, very early one of our D.I.'s had attempted to teach us how to change step if, somehow, we found ourselves out of step. But when a lot of these characters tried that changing step they'd fall flat on their faces. Our D.I. told us that when a guy fell down just to march right over him. In fact he said, "Step on him and as you go over him give him a kick in the uh, give him a kick in the head, or anywhere." You can imagine where he said.

After we'd sorta learned how to march around and do a few elementary movements, such as squads right, and squads left, column right and column left, we were told to bring our rifles with us the next time we had a formation.

They proceeded to teach us the Manual of Arms. That was how to handle those guns. I MEAN, rifles or pieces. There was a right and left shoulder arms, port arms, order arms and how to give a salute with that piece. In the process several of us dang near got our brains busted out when some awkward nut would let his piece get away from him altogether and before it'd hit the ground usually it knocked several guys on the head before it ever got to the ground. Any time this happened, the poor boy who had it happen to him usually had to do several laps around the parade ground at double time and he'd certainly have to sleep with his piece that night. That was just about absolutely certain. Other little innovations might be and often were added to the above. Whatever happened to suggest itself to the D.I.!

After we had sorta gotten to the point that we could handle those weapons we were taught to do "Physical Drill With Arms." This was a kind of calisthenics where we shoved that rifle straight out in front at arms length, then back to our chests then above our heads with the muzzle pointing ahead of us then switch and put the butt end of it in front. Then we'd bend over and touch the sling part to our toes and back and forth—by the numbers.

Soon after we'd gotten to master that we'd do it silently—without any numbers, going through a whole routine of this magnificent calisthenics almost without a sound.

I expect that you have already guessed that any number of us got whacked over the heads with somebody else's rifle. Rifles got dropped, and various ones had to perform some mighty special duties as a result.

Then, as an added attraction, our beloved D.I.'s had us fix bayonets. That amounted to attaching the bayonet to the end of the rifle. That made the whole business weigh around 10 pounds. That still ain't very heavy, is it? Well, no, not until you did physical drill with arms for about 30 minutes or so. Then the cussed thing began feeling as if it weighed about a hundred pounds.

If you know me personally and you've been wondering whether Mama might have dropped me on my head when I's a baby, she didn't. What happened to me was getting hit over the head several times with a rifle which ain't very conducive to much brightness. That also can cause a fellow to be a might gun-shy.

But in spite of all the hazards most of us learned the manual of arms, how to march and do close order drill and a few other odds and ends which were customarily taught to boots, or recruits, in the Marines.

One afternoon we were doing close order drill and were given this command, "On Right Front Into Line, March." This was a maneuver where each squad leader had to give his squad commands independently so as to change direction of the entire platoon and bring them up on a line facing to the right of the way we had been going.

Well, sir, the runt squad was the last to have to make any move. John Glowa's first command of squads right was just fine, and we marched off a short distance; then he should have given us a "Squads left" command. Instead, he yells out "Squads right." This was the preparatory command. Before he gave us the command of execution I told him that he'd have us all marching off in the wrong direction and that we would all get our ends chewed out. I told him this in plenty of time for him to change his command to the proper one before he gave that command of execution.

He didn't do it! Went ahead and gave his command of execution and as I'd told him there we went streaking off in the opposite direction and, sure enough, Corporal Peck called us all a bunch of dumb you can guess whats. Then he had us do about a dozen laps around the field—double time.

That afternoon just before we were dismissed to get ready for chow he asked that all the squad leaders step out and join him. John Glowa was right in amongst em.

After chow, friend (?) Glowa told me that I was to report to Corporal Peck's room and take my rifle with me. I did, and in about three or four more minutes six more guys joined me. When the seven of us were assembled he told us that it had been reported to him that we had been "talking in ranks."

We all knew that this was a definite no no. We'd known that from the very beginning. And I also knew that Glowa had reported me to Peck for what I'd said to him when he was about to march us off in the wrong direction that afternoon.

Peck told us to begin doing physical drill with arms. After we'd finished doing the whole sequence he informed us to just continue until he told us to stop.

Now this was when, after about 30 minutes or more, that those 8.69 pound pieces began to feel that they weighed a ton. We all kept this up while Peck sat there as unconcerned as a cucumber and read.

Finally one of the boys just passed out. Collapsed. He tried to get up. He couldn't make it. Then another collapsed. When there were just two of us left, another guy and me, Peck told us to go back to our barracks.

When we got back we were just barely able to make it up the steps to our bunks. For a solid month after that I believe every muscle in my body ached every time I moved.

However, I didn't do any more talking in ranks. No Siree. No matter what.

The morning we were to leave Parris Island I went over to John Glowa and I told him, "Ole boy, I hope I run into you somewhere out in the Corps. I've a score to settle with you."

It was much too late for him to report me to the D.I. again, and I knew it. He knew it too. John was sent to the F.M.F. (Fleet Marine Force) at Quantico, Virginia. I went to Sea School at Norfolk Navy Yard, Portsmouth, Virginia, and we didn't see each other again for about two years.

But I finally caught up with him.

NEMO THE BEAST

Before I take you to the happy reunion of my dear old friend, John Glowa—remember my tattletale, pigeon stooling squad leader?—I must tell you about our hanging out clothes at Parris Island while I was still in Boot Camp.

Immediately after supper each day we all took baths. We were instructed to take extra good ones. All over baths. And would you believe that one of our D.I.'s actually inspected us afterward? Oh yeah! They'd look at our ankles, necks, around our ears and *in* them. If they found any evidence that we'd neglected any of these parts they just naturally assumed we had been sorta negligent about the rest of the body. Then he would direct that four other boots take the culprit and give him a G.I. bath.

A G.I. bath consisted of the four washers taking their stiff bristle brushes and plenty of soap and scrubbing this jerk from his head to toe. I mean to tell you that they were told to wash him ALL OVER—EVERYWHERE.

After only one of these beauty treatments, to my knowledge, no man ever required the second one. And I know this will surprise you to learn that I escaped this treatment. Nope, I didn't have any "ring around the collar."

Then after our baths we all fell out and gathered around the scrubbing benches. And we proceeded to wash our clothes. Those who were real happy with their new lives would sing the old nursery rhyme, "This is the way we wash our clothes." Actually, the only ones who ever sang that were the ones who were a little less than thorough, conscientious, and cleanliness minded.

When the clothes were all done, and there were just very few minutes allotted for this, a D.I. would blow a whistle and then we would line up under the clothes lines and wait for our beloved D.I. to come and inspect our handiwork. He knew just the places to look.

Now that first day was sumpin else. This one clown, Corporal Peck, was the very worst at this job. Seemed that he took a fiendish delight in snarling at a pore scared recruit and saying, "You miserable &%X$#&XX*+%, I see nicotine on your skivvies. Somebody's been blowing smoke up your $%X#X. Turn your bucket upside down." Of course, all those freshly washed clothes hit the cotton pickin' dirt. Then, he'd say, "Now kick dirt all over em and then stomp em." Naturally, this messed em up good and proper. But the D.I. knew how to remedy that. He sent the offender back to the wash rack to scrub his clothes again. Good this time.

While this extra scrubbing was taking place, the rest of us had to wait until everybody was ready to hang clothes. Then we got that whistle again and AGAIN we fell out under the clothes line. You guessed it. There were very few who had to undergo this routine the second time. And those of us who had been lucky enough to get by without having to re-do our own learned pretty fast.

When we had sorta mastered the art of the manual of arms (handling our rifles) both on the march and standing still plus how to do a reasonable fascimile of marching, or close order drill we began studying some little pamphlets on our rifles—range, windage, and elevation. Incidentally, that piece was a .30 caliber Springfield, model 1918. And they were mighty accurate weapons. I mean pieces.

We were taught the firing positions of standing, or offhand, sitting, kneeling, and prone. Now this standing or off-hand position was what I had most of my problems with. This was used at 200 yards range. I did a little better with the kneeling position but not much. At 200 yards we had to hold that rifle up there and shoot at a six-inch bull's eye. One would think that with that big a target a body'd be able to bust it wide open every shot.

But not so. Most of us, when we assumed that position, that gun, I mean PIECE, would wobble and stray all over the entire target. That's when we were told that the thing to do was take up the slack in the trigger and then begin to squeeze it slowly, and tenderly, and when we saw that bull's eye as that muzzle waved around and around and up and down and sideways, to finish squeezing the shot on off. Now this was just the easiest thing in the world to do when we were dry firing—you know, practicing without any ammunition. We were all sure that we'd make EXPERT when we got on that rifle range and really began doing some real shooting. After all, I'd shot 22 rifles, shot guns, and pistols at home, in the C.M.T.C., and the National Guard. And, if we shot expert that would raise our pay $5.00 a month. Expert was a score of 315 out of 350. If we managed to make sharpshooter that would raise our pay $3.00. And, Man, when your base pay was $21.00 a month, that extra pay was a powerful incentive.

We all heard of a character out at the rifle range, a fellow who ran the butts. Now, the butts were where the targets were. They were pasted up on a rack arrangement and it took two men to operate each one.

Won't ever forget that bum; no, that MANIAC, who was in charge of the pits, or the butts. The first day we were taken out there to meet him. No, it wasn't what one might call a formal introduction. In other words, we didn't get to shake his hand or anything of that sort. Our three D.I.'s went along with us. I think the reason that all three of them went along was on account of they probably thought that some of us might take off for the tall timbers when we saw Nemo the Beast.

Now Nemo the Beast was somewhat larger than Liverlip Gordon. The only clothes he wore, that we could be certain of, was a pair of overalls, shoes, and a very battered campaign hat. Maybe he had socks on, and skivvies, but they were not visible. We were told that he was Corporal Nemo and that he was in charge of the pits. Corporal Sharit told us that some people called him Nemo the Beast, but he advised that we were to call him CORPORAL Nemo. I sure hoped that I didn't ever need to call him.

Nemo lumbered and waddled around as if he might stumble with his next step. But he was the fastest big man I had ever seen, and the rest of the platoon felt the same way and besides his being big, fat, and hairy as an ape, he was mean. He waddled out in front of us with a long tree limb in his hand. He said that he would tell us how to operate "them &/sp!/sn%$#7$% targets" and between spitting every other breath he proceeded to give us a talking to. It had nothing whatsoever to do with the proper operation of those targets. It consisted of his cussin us out and explaining what that tree limb was for. I'd already imagined what he would do with that.

When he yelled, "Ready on the right, ready on the left, TARGETS," we were to hoist em up, and woe be unto the one who didn't get em up fast enough to suit the beast. Same applied if they didn't come down fast enough to suit him, or if we didn't get em marked right or pasted up rapidly enough. Sometimes he would just come by and, just to keep us very alert, he'd whack Hell out of us with that tree limb.

When we were initially introduced, he did explain to us about the disks which we used to signal the shooters. A big white one meant a bull's eye, the black one meant a four, a black and white checkered one meant a three and a half black and half white one meant a deuce, or a two. There were no ones. And then if there were not a full 10 shots on the target, we waived a big red flag which Nemo said was "Maggie's drawers" and meant that the shooter had slap missed the whole target. Of course all his explanations were generously sprinkled with obscenities, vulgarities, and a heap o' cussin.

There wasn't a man in my platoon who escaped Nemo's anger. I didn't escape it three different times. And I'm a-telling you, when Nemo the Bas——, I mean BEAST, hit ye with his persuader, you could see the red whelps for weeks and feel them for days.

Several of us discussed taking some live ammo to the butts with us and shooting him between the eyes and just telling God that the pore old feller died of a splitting headache, and we talked of telling our D.I.'s that he'd just died of natural causes. Natural causes? Why, if you'd just been exposed to Nemo the Beast, you'd certainly have agreed that we all felt that he had given us all a natural cause to kill him.

I promise that I'll give you an account of John Glowa's and my reunion. Ain't room just here—and besides I wanted yawl to meet Nemo the Beast.

DAY OF RETRIBUTION

After putting my time in aboard the USS Texas, 26 months, I was due for shore duty. There was a little ritual that went along with this request for duty on land. It consisted of my being called into the first sergeant's office and told to list my preferences—1, 2, 3.

My first choice was Pensacola on account of that was so near home. No. two was Charleston, W. Va. Ammunition Depot. I told the sarge that I'd just leave the third one blank because after those two mentioned I just didn't much care where they sent me. He said, "Why, just write in Parris Island." I felt like smacking him in the teeth. But he was bigger than I. However, I did tell him that when I had left that place after Boot Camp that I didn't EVER want to see it again. He laughed and said, "Well, it isn't likely that you will. It's just that I thought we should put down a third choice."

When my orders came, they were for Parris Island, S.C., Recruit Depot.!

So, I was going back!

On reporting in I was assigned as an assistant drill instructor. I worked with that D.I. a couple or three weeks, and then was reassigned to another with a platoon in a different phase of their training. Then to a couple others, one of which was a platoon on the rifle range.

There, as usual, was Nemo the Beast running up and down the line whacking the daylights out of pore recruits with his wicked tree limb. To say the least, he was a mighty repulsive, mean, brutal monster. I felt that the chief drill instructor should have intervened on behalf of the recruits. But none of them ever did. Nemo was sure IN CHARGE.

I couldn't help but remember the three times he had hit me with his tree limb. The third time he hit me I had the misfortune of facing him when he hit me. The end of one of the switches on his limb hit me in the corner of my right eye and busted the bark on my cheek. My eye was bloody red, and I just didn't see very much with it the rest of the time in boot camp.

I made myself a small promise to the effect that if I was ever a Chief D.I. that he wouldn't do my recruits any such way. At the time I had no idea just how I would, or even if I could, prevent that, but I certainly did intend to make an effort.

Shortly I was given a platoon of my own, at least one to take through training. And I'll tell you for sure that I dreaded the rifle range and Nemo the Beast. But, like it or not, it had to be dealt with.

In no time at all, it seemed to me, my platoon was on the range, and I knew that that promise I'd made to myself had to be kept . . . that about not allowing Nemo to treat them like some inanimate objects, or worse.

We were marching from the Main Station out to the range one afternoon and on this march my feeble mind was working like crazy in an effort to formulate some plan. Finally it dawned on me.

I didn't have to consult with an assistant because mine had had to go to the hospital for something. I had those lads all to myself, and there wasn't anyone to help with them, nobody, nothing—just me.

After supper that first night I called a formation and then had them all fall out and form a semi-circle around me. I had them all sitting down. I told them they could smoke if they liked. None of them knew what was coming. This was a brand new situation for all of them. I thought that some of them were a little apprehensive.

Anyhow, I told them that I wanted them to keep quiet and listen very closely to what I had to say to them. They did. A few lit cigarettes.

I began. "Boys, when you go into those pits tomorrow, you will encounter Nemo the Beast. He is in charge. He runs the show down there. And if any of you have thought I was rough on you, then you have a rude awakening coming to you. He weighs around 300 pounds and is well over six feet tall. His chief entertainment in life, I think, is running up and down the lines with a long heavy tree limb in his hand and knocking Hell out of recruits. If he thinks you aren't moving fast enough he'll hit you, or if you don't do exactly what he's told you, in just the exact way, he will let you have it. Or for no reason at all.''

I told them about my having experienced his brutality first hand and the fact that I came very near to losing an eye because of him and his tree limb.

I instructed them to do their jobs as best they could and told them that if they didn't do that then they would be in trouble with me. None of them wanted any part of that either. I pointed out to them that they were not to stand facing the Beast, regardless, because I certainly did not want any of them to perhaps lose an eye. So, they had a tough job on their hands—that of working those targets plus keeping an eye on Nemo all the time when he was anywhere in their vicinity.

And more. "Before tomorrow is done, the chances are that each of you will be hit at least once with that limb, so do your jobs and do not let him get a lick at your face. Now, when we get all through down there tomorrow I will get you in formation to march you out of the pits. Only we aren't going out immediately. As soon as you're all lined up, I will blow my whistle and when that happens, I want you to break formation as fast as you can move, and I want the biggest guys to pounce on Nemo. I want EVERYONE OF YOU to get to him somehow if you possibly can and get the Beast on the ground.''

That very first platoon I had was composed mostly of six footers, or close to it.

After telling them that I wanted them to get Nemo down on the ground, I paused long enough to let that really sink in. I looked all around at their faces. Most were very somber. Then a few of them smiled.

"If any of you are worried about the possibility of any court martial or anything else, forget it. If anything happens about this, I'll be the one who gets it because I'm giving you direct orders that I fully expect to be carried out to the letter.'' A few more faces brightened up.

I continued, "When you get him down on the ground, I want his tree limb taken away from him by whoever can get his hands on it. Then I want his overall jacket ripped off him and then I want his overalls jerked down around his ankles. Then I want two big men on each arm and two more on each foot. I want him spread eagled and naked from the top of his head to his ankles."

Again I hesitated and looked around the group. I couldn't find but a couple or three men who hadn't begun to smile all over themselves.

"When he is properly arranged, then I want you to get in line and as it comes your turn I want you to take that tree limb and bust his backside with all your might. If he has hit you twice or more, then give him a swarp for each lick he has meted out to you. Now if there is anyone of you who feels that you would prefer not to take part in this, I want you to remain after this formation, and I will talk with you PERSONALLY." This must have sounded a little ominous to them. I intended it to.

Then I asked if they all had clearly understood what the plan was, and, if so, I wanted to hear an answer. I never before heard such a thundering ear-splitting "YES, SIR!"

To a man they were ready. Then I detailed the biggest eight men to hold onto his arms and legs. They knew exactly who they were and just what they were to do. Before dismissing them, I cautioned them to keep quiet about our plans.

The next morning was electric with excitement. I could feel it in my very bones. I reminded them that before the "operation" began that they would have to take their lumps from Nemo but told them also that they'd have their chance before lunch time that day. I asked them if they were ready. Again a mighty loud "YES, SIR."

Those boys could hardly wait to get to the pits and see Nemo. In an instant, after laying eyes on him and seeing the tree limb in his hand, they knew I had not lied to them.

For some unknown reason that day Nemo was more vicious, more brutal that I could ever remember. I thought to myself, "Lay it on, Ole Boy; you're just laying up treasures in Heaven for yourself."

Finally the job in the pits was over, and I believe that Nemo had waited on every man, some twice or more. I said, "Fall in." They got in formation. Then I blew the whistle on Nemo. Some 60 men pounced on him, or all tried. But he was down!

In nothing flat his jacket had been ripped off and his overalls were down around his ankles. The men got in line. And most of them had to use two hands to handle that limb. But handle it they most assuredly did.

As they worked on Nemo, I was kneeling down at his head and he was cursing me first and threatening me with a court martial. I told him that if I did get court martialed it would be the most interesting one ever held on that island on account of his brutality to recruits.

Then Nemo began to invoke the name of God. I told him that I was extremely surprised that he and the Lord were on speaking terms. "But," I said, "Nemo, you so and so, you can pray all you want to but I'm the one who is gonna answer your prayers today!"

After the praying bit didn't help Nemo, he began hollering, screaming and crying. Finally all the men had satisfied their taste for blood and then I took my turn. I had to use two hands to wield the limb or what was left of it. It was seasoned mighty good and there were even some pretty good switches left on it. I told Nemo to look at me because I had something else to tell him. He could just barely turn his face toward me. When he did, I gave him one powerful whack right across his face. I reminded him what that was for.

When the job was complete, I gave him a swift kick in the rear and told him to get on his feet and pull his britches up. He somehow made it. Then I told him to walk around some. He barely could. Before I left the pits, which was shortly afterward, I told Nemo that I never wanted to see his tree limb again and if I ever heard of his hitting another recruit with anything that I'd be back after him. He must have believed me because that ended the brutality in the pits.

Although I had cautioned my recruits to keep their mouths shut, the news was just too good to keep. By that night everyone on the rifle range knew about it and when I went in to the main station, the news had preceded me. Old Salts (Ole timers) and everybody I came in contact with was congratulating me for having "Tended to Nemo the Beast."

Incidentally, I never heard the first word about any Court Martial.

THE REUNION

As I told you, after Boot Camp, I went to Sea School and my Boot Camp squad leader, John Glowa, went to the F.M.F.—Fleet Marine Force. We had lost sight of one another for a matter of a couple of years. And some mighty important things happened during that time.

Four of us from my recruit platoon went to Sea School on account of we had been selected as a result of some tests we'd taken and their results. The grades indicated to somebody that we might have sense enough to make it to the U.S. Naval Academy. So, it was necessary that we have some sea schooling. Then it was required that we have nine months sea duty before taking the entrance exams for the academy.

After only three weeks of that schooling they transferred us to the USS Texas to begin getting that nine months of sea duty.

We didn't get any preferential treatment because we were candidates for possible admission to the academy. In fact, I believe that we were handled mighty roughly because we were, maybe, gonna get a crack at Annapolis. No, we just had to do a sight of studying besides our regular tours of duty.

In a few months after going aboard the Texas, I got a promotion to PFC—Private First Class. That raised my pay to $30 a month. Then, in just a couple more months, darned if I didn't get another big raise in pay with a promotion to CORPORAL and a whopping $42.00 a month! Yeah, and since I was then a non com—non-commissioned officer—they issued me red stripes to have sewn on the legs of my trousers.

And I'da given near bout anything back then if we'd had color film so's I could have had dozens of pictures made of myself in them red-striped britches. Talk about proud! I purely wuz!

Not long after I got this fabulous promotion, we got word that we'd be picking up five or six hundred FMF Marines and that we would participate in maneuvers in the Caribbean. These FMF boys were gonna practice their landing parties and assaulting enemy beachheads.

It'd be impossible for you to imagine how eager I was for those Quantico Marines to come aboard. You see, I's excited about the possibilities of, maybe, some of my old Boot Camp buddies being among em. And there was ONE in particular in whom I was so extremely interested. John Glowa.

After they came aboard quite a number of additional guard duty posts were assigned and the Texas Marines were in charge of same. By this time I had already been designated as a sergeant of the guard which meant that I was in charge of all the guards on the starboard shift. And after the FMF boys came aboard they sure added a bunch of new guard posts.

Soon as the FMF first sergeant made out the guard roster, he sent it down to me. I grabbed it and began reading all those names, and I want ye to know that the name PRIVATE JOHN GLOWA just about leaped out and slapped me in the eyes. Right away my ole mouf was justa watering. I could taste VENGEANCE.

Boot Camp Good Buddy Glowa was scheduled to do the 8 to 12 watch down in the bag alley. This was a compartment down about three decks in the belly of that battlewagon. In it was a short distance of about 50 feet, and it did actually have a lot of sea bags stored along one wall or bulkhead.

The ship's marines also had the corporals of the guard so I knew I wasn't about to get any flak from them. So when the FMF boys reported to our compartment I just stayed out of sight because I wanted my dearly beloved boot camp buddy to be COMPLETELY surprised when we met. And we were slap gonna meet pretty soon after he went on post.

After about an hour I went to the O.D. (Officer of the Deck), stood rigidly at attention and when he turned to me I saluted him and said, "Sir, permission to inspect the guard below decks." He returned my salute and replied, "Permission granted."

I went straight to the bag alley and saw my good ole buddy sitting flat on his rear in a hatchway or doorway, and he was smoking a big cigar and reading one of those old 10 cent western magazines.

Now, besides the 12 general orders that applied to every guard post there were also special orders which applied to different posts. Each time a guard was posted he was supposed to familiarize himself with what the special orders were and where a list of them was posted.

First off I asked, "Marine, what are the special orders for this post?" He was a tough FMF Marine and he told me that he didn't know nor did he give a "¢%7$3$#!"

I informed him that he wasn't walking his post in any military manner nor was he observing ANYTHING in sight or hearing. Also told him of another general order or 2 that he was violating. Then I told him that one of his special orders was that he was supposed to prevent anyone's smoking anywhere on his post because there was always the danger of fire. I pointed out several other things to him.

During the course of my informing him about all his violations while on guard, he was getting mighty powerfully insolent with me. And that was a no-no if there ever was one. Nobody, but NOBODY, was ever supposed to be insolent to his superior officer. He called me a few names along with his insolence.

I spoke just as softly to him—just as Sergeant Watson had to us in Boot Camp. And at that particular moment I believe that I had just as much venom in my mind as our old D.I. Watson ever did. Probably more because I had a heap of "getting even" to do.

After listening to this jerk and remembering real good all over again about the night I had done physical drill with arms until I was barely able to move just because I'd actually tried to help the dumb clown, I went to a phone within a few feet of Private Glowa and called for the Corporal of the Guard to get the supernumerary—a standby guard—and come to the bag alley post.

Incidentally, Glowa had worked his way all the way up from buck private to PRIVATE.

Glowa wanted to know why I was making that phone call. I gently explained to him that I was having him relieved of his post. More flak.

In about five minutes his relief showed up with the Corporal of the Guard. I ordered Glowa to turn his gun and belt over to that man and then I told him that he was under arrest.

He still hadn't recognized me. I didn't help him out any with that problem.

The Corporal of the Guard and I marched him to the O.D., and I explained to him the reasons I had arrested the man. I also asked the O.D. what I should do with him. The O.D. was a dandy! He said, "You have the keys to the brig. Lock him up! Have him at Captain's mast tomorrow morning at 0900." (9 a.m. to those who may be uninformed.)

On the way back to the brig John finally recognized me and began pleading and begging me as his "ole boot camp buddy." I let him know that I wasn't his buddy from anywhere. He commenced telling me that that would keep him from making PFC. I extended him a world of sympathy. Oh yeah! I almost cried with John, but not for the same reasons.

At Captain's mast the next morning I had my culprit in front of the old man. Captain Emmet was about 6 ft. 4, real thin, and he wore his bifocals about half way down his nose. He started right off with "my man." He said, "Corporal, what is this man charged with?"

I read off the long list of infractions, violations, misdemeanors, AND the felonies. Then Cap'n Emmet looked at Glowa and asked, "Young man, what do you have to say for yourself?"

John began, "Well, Sir," and that's as far as he got when the Cap'n interrupted him. He stared very hard at buck private Glowa and said, "10 days bread and water and you can have it in solitary confinement!"

Now when a man was sent to solitary confinement and on bread and water, there was a procedure that had to be followed. We had to take him to sick bay (hospital part) for him to be examined and for the doctor to determine if the man were physically able to stand it. They weighed him also. The doctor took a look at John and told me to take him to the brig. Nobody ever received such glad tidings as those were to me.

The solitary confinement cell of the brig was sort of an iron box with just barely enough room to cuss a cat in without getting hair in your teeth. The prisoner was allowed one blanket and that's all he had between him and the cold hard steel. Nothing else. At each meal time he got one slice of bread and a cup of water. Every third day he got full rations.

After John was safely locked up in his little cubicle, I had him get on his tiptoes and stick the end of his nose out the highest hole he could reach. I had some things to tell him. I told him just why he was in there! Reminded him!

There's more to the story. Read on.

TIGHTENING THE SCREWS

When the FMF Marines came aboard, they called us seagoing marines "Seagoing Bellhops." That generated a very valuable bit of mighty useful animosity between the two groups. Anyhow it worked just fine for my purposes—my plans for Buck Private Glowa.

The USS Texas Marines were in charge of the guard. We were, in effect, the ship's policemen. When there was no one in the brig, we could always "secure the watch." That meant that those boys who were scheduled for that post could just stay in the compartment; they were just on stand-by.

But with a "dangerous criminal" in custody then the brig watch had to go on duty. So, soon as I had John Glowa safely hemmed up in his comfy little hole, I took our brig watch man just a few feet away from the door so that Glowa couldn't hear what I told him.

Among those instructions were that he was to keep Glowa on his toes. Standing on his tiptoes with his nose stuck in the highest hole he could reach in that iron door. To make sure of which hole the brig watch and I went inside and had Glowa demonstrate. Why, that punk could darn near reach the top row of holes!

Also told the guard that he was to keep him there for as long as Glowa could hold it. I knew that wasn't gonna be too long; however, I told the guard that if he had any sass out of Glowa about that nose in the hole-tiptoe business to go in there with his night stick or billy club and work him over. I said this in Glowa's hearing.

I stayed down below to personally supervise the tip-toeing and nose-holing for a while. I don't remember just how long Ole John was able to hold this top hole, but seems that it was almost an hour.

The first time he eased it down to a lower hole, the brig watch banged on the door and ordered him to "get that nose back in its hole."

Now as for the brig watch going in the cell to "work Glowa over" with that stick, I knew he'd never have to do any such thing. It was very obvious that that Leatherneck Marine Glowa was completely subdued and also that he fully believed that I would personally see to it that he got everything I'd promised him. And he had already been in the Marines long enough to have heard some wild and wooly yarns about how an unruly prisoner could and often did get treated while doing time in the brig.

I had my buddies in the ship's Marine detachment help me think up all sorts of new methods of torturing this jerk. That is, without leaving any visible marks on his hide. Of course, the old nose in the hole bit was a very tried, true, and tested method of inflicting a little bit of torture. However, I wanted some innovations.

Wound up with a multitude of em.

One was to see that he didn't get too much sleep. The brig watch had orders to flick the light on in Glowa's cell every few minutes and yell at him, "Standby for inspection!" Glowa had to hit the deck at a stiff ramrod attention. I wanted the ole boy to have a heap of sore muscles just as I had had them because of him.

And for "soring" up muscles, there ain't nothing that can beat doing push-ups until you fall on your face. Then sit-ups until he couldn't raise his head and I had him count them out loud. And I was always very fond of duck waddling with his fingers laced behind his head. So, he did an amazing amount of duck waddling.

Between my detachment buddies and me, we worked out some mindboggling exercises for him, and they were all very cooperative and eager to help me administer and supervise Glowa's exercising. When each new brig watch came on duty, I had him instructed to have ole Glow worm hit that nosehole and while there tell him in every detail the incident that took place at Parris Island, just what he told our D.I. on me and the pain and torture he had caused me. Then he had to go through a routine of telling how sorry he was he'd done such a thing, and all about his understanding just how I had reason to see that he was punished good and proper.

What we did was a little old-fashioned brain washing on this jerk.

There was no question about it; he suffered for his sin.

Any time he heard a noise outside his cell, he would immediately get on his feet and make an effort to get his nose in the hole. Sure, he passed out several times from sheer exhaustion and fright. And I made sure that he had plenty of reason to be both scared and tired. Bone tired.

Any time we had a man or men in the brig, even in solitary confinement, it was customary to take them out daily and up on top side to give them some exercise. Walk them about and stretch their muscles. And, ordinarily, prisoners looked forward to this brief respite. However, I can assure you that Buck Private Glowa DID NOT look forward to it! He didn't want anything like exercise. He wanted REST!

I mentioned to him, asked him, several times if he would like to talk with the Chaplain, but I did that in such a way that he knew I wasn't about to let him get anywhere near any chaplain. So, he always answered in the negative when I made any Chaplain's suggestion.

Well, at least, I did inquire of him as to his desires in the spiritual realm.

Finally, he completed his 10 days on cake and wine—bread and water. Some of the guys had another name for it, but it'd be a no-no in print.

When the time came for him to be let out, I went to the brig and escorted him to sick bay. He had to be checked over by the ship's doctor and weighed. The pore sonofagun could hardly walk. I was so sorry for him.

He had lost an unusual amount of weight and the doctor asked him about it. Glowa began telling him the worst kinda story anybody ever listened to. I let him do all of his telling. And lemme assure you if that doctor had believed him, I would have still been in Portsmouth Naval Prison.

When Glowa got all through his story-telling, the doctor turned to me and he said, "Corporal, is there anything to what this man has said?" I replied, "Why, Hell No, Sir! This man is a born liar. I was with him in Boot Camp in Parris Island, and I know him from away back and nobody can put any dependence in anything he says."

With that the doctor told him to get back to his unit. As Glowa was leaving, I had him wait just a second for me to tell him something. I told him that I, along with every seagoing bellhop aboard the USS Texas would have an eye on him as long as he stayed on that ship, and we'd all be hoping we could catch him again so I could take him back to Captain's Mast.

Then I dismissed him.

I saw him several times after that, and he always had a real wild-cowed look as if he expected me to pounce right on him and eat him alive.

I GET MEAN

A few days ago a friend asked why I had waited so long to write the stories about my involvement in the United States Marine Corps. I had to tell him that my only reason had to be that many of those experiences were not very pleasant and certainly did not reflect very much enhancement on the Corps. Also, I told him that my having been a Marine sure didn't do any good for the outfit.

Actually a lot of the things that happened, where I was involved, would sort of make me look bad. Nobody likes that aspect of a situation. However, I decided to write them and just let the chips fall where they may.

I mentioned my returning to Parris Island, South Carolina, U.S. Marine Corps Recruit Depot; also that that was a place I never wanted to set eyes on again as long as I lived. That's what I had said to myself many a time, especially for the first little while after leaving there from Boot Camp.

When I learned that I was indeed going back and that I would be a D.I. (Drill Instructor), I thought, "Oh, my Lord, me a D.I.—not in a million years." But in those days you went where they said and did what you were told and that was it. Or ELSE.

I was first assigned to a Sergeant Milner as an assistant. He was an "Old Timer," a Shanghai Marine, and he'd been involved in a few skirmishes in Nicaragua, had a bunch of hash marks on his sleeve, plus he wore a pretty nice collection of ribbons on his chest. He had an air of competence about him. I hoped that some of the latter would rub off on me because I flat didn't know what I was doing. And, furthermore, I didn't even want to do it.

Right off the bat I'd made up my mind that I certainly would not treat recruits in any way such as I had been treated when I was in their boots.

After following Sgt. Milner and the platoon around for a few days, suddenly he informed me that he wanted me to fall em out and march them to chow. I was shaking in my shoes. However, I did just that and when we got back from chow, he met me just as I was dismissing them. He told me in no uncertain terms that he had watched me and the platoon and he wasn't at all pleased with the way I handled them. Said they were a bunch of raw_ _ _ _ d civilians and that it was our job to make Marines out of them. He told me that it was mighty obvious that I was scared, and he told me that those recruits knew it and unless I began giving my commands in an authoritative voice and giving em hell when they loused things up, I'd never make the grade.

To tell you the truth, I wasn't the least bit interested in "making the grade" as he called it. In fact, I was hoping that somebody would recognize that fact and decide to transfer me to the supply room or some other place where I wouldn't be expected to maltreat recruits.

You guessed it. In no time at all I began hollering at them pore kids. KIDS? Why, very few of them were younger than I. But Milner had convinced me that I had better act tough and do my best to look that way, regardless of how I felt about the matter.

A few weeks passed and more men were brought in to become D.I.'s. The war in Europe was already underway, and the Marines, along with the other military services, were slowly beginning to beef up their forces.

When I joined the Marines, there were more New York City policemen than there were U.S. Marines. So, we, along with the other branches of the service, were due some "beefing-up."

When about 20 new D.I.'s had come in, we were all ordered to report to the office of Col. Louis R. Jones, Commanding Officer of Recruit Depot. When we were all gathered in a room adjacent to his office, he came in to talk with us. He gave us to understand what our jobs were—that of making Marines out of raw civilians. He impressed upon us that it wasn't an easy job. He said a lot of other things, all peppered with quite a few salty, caustic, and explicit little profanities.

The colonel was a real old timer and had "come up through the ranks." He had gotten a battlefield commission during WW I and had managed to hang in there and make it all the way up to a colonel's rank. He was tough and he knew his job and he didn't intend to tolerate anyone who didn't reflect his own philosophy regarding training, or, as he put it, "Making G.D. tough Marines."

As he closed his remarks to us, he reached up and grabbed his long black cigar which he'd had clinched between his teeth and said, "If I find as many as ONE recruit who likes his drill instructor, I'll bust you and transfer you to hell out of here. You can't do the job I want done and have your recruits like you! Now, do you gentlemen understand what I have told you?" We assured him that we did.

Among those of us in there meeting with the Old Man were only a couple of PFC's and the rest of us were corporals and sergeants. Not a man wanted to lose the few stripes of ratings that he had. We had all worked too hard to get them, and I'm sure that all of us left his office with a resolve to make sure that our recruits hated our guts.

I went back to where my platoon was quartered and for no reason at all I had them fall out. As soon as they were in formation and the squad leaders had reported, I told them in the harshest language I knew that I'd give them exactly five minutes to roll a heavy marching order (heavy packs) and fall out. I knew that they couldn't possibly do it in that short time, but I had just gotten the colonel's message and I intended to waste no time in my "gettin' em to hate me campaign."

When they got in formation at the end of that five minute period, I do believe that was the sorriest looking bunch of bedraggled looking critters that I'd ever seen. They were all in various degrees of dress and undress. Only four or five actually had their packs strapped to their backs and, well, they were just a heckuva looking mess.

For several minutes I practiced on chewing em out for the fouled up looking mess they were in. Then I told em I'd give em five more minutes to get back in their barracks and get those packs rolled and told them that when I blew the whistle again I wanted to see them all out there but that this time they were to fall out with their rifles and fixed bayonets.

It's a thousand wonders that someone hadn't got bayonetted on the way back out of that building. I sent them back the third time and told them that I wouldn't blow any whistle. I wanted to see just how long it would take them to do those simple things.

I stood outside the barracks and waited on them. They could all see me from inside and I made a big to-do about looking at my watch. In all the confusion some came out without their rifles, some had forgotten their packs, and some had removed their bayonets. It was a mess. I remember that one poor fellow came out with just one shoe on.

I had them to open ranks for "inspection." There wasn't a single man who was ready for any kind of inspection. This gave me much more practice in "chewin' out."

Again I sent them back in to secure (put up) their rifles and fall back out. Then I had them "police up" (clean up) the area. Only I imposed a small condition or requirement on this. They had to do it in a duck-waddling position. I told them to pick up everything bigger than a pinhead.

By the time I turned them loose, I was absolutely sure that not a man in that platoon had any kind of feeling for me except extreme hatred. First of all the area didn't need any kind of cleaning up. And their doing all that duck waddling was about as useful as the fifth wheel on a wagon. They hadn't gotten to write any letters home, they hadn't been able to go to the PX to buy any pogey bait (candy, milkshakes, cigarettes). Nothing. They just barely had time to get their baths and get into bed before lights out.

I'd betcha one thing. If Col. Jones had talked with any of my recruits that night they'd have all convinced him that they hated me. REAL GOOD.

THE HURRICANE

It was on a Sunday, August 11, 1940. When I awakened and looked outside, it looked as if we'd have a dreary day. It suited my mood because I wasn't too happy about having to spend the weekend on the post. Parris Island had never been my idea of the most ideal place to enjoy.

The skies looked ominous and the breeze that was blowing just seemed to bear an evil portent. And before I got my platoon of recruits back to their barracks from breakfast, it had begun to come a gentle rain. The winds were beginning to take on much more wallop. Things simply didn't look right.

There were some old World War I "shotgun" barracks that were being used because of the build-up in the Marine Corps just before we were to get into WW II. They were long narrow buildings and each one looked as if it should have been torn down years before. They just didn't appear to be very substantial. My platoon was quartered in the first of four of these double decker cracker boxes, nearest the Main Station.

As the morning wore on, all these weather conditions began increasing in intensity. It had all the appearances of a mighty big blow, and soon the winds began to rattle the old barracks.

I tried to write some letters but couldn't think of anything to write except that the weather looked bad and I felt uneasy. Then I tried to read a book but somehow I couldn't concentrate for looking out the windows.

The more looking out I did the worse the weather looked—and got! The trees that I could see were being pushed around and their tops bent toward the ground. Shortly the wind seemed to be changing directions so that those trees were getting twisted in first one direction and then another. The rain was coming down in torrents.

Sometime around 9:00 I saw a car coming toward our barracks. I recognized it as our Training Officer's car. He was a Major E. J. Farron.

I got out to his car by the time he set foot on the ground and asked him about the possibility of moving my men out of those old barracks. I told him that it looked as if this weather deal was going to develop into a full blown hurricane and that I didn't believe that our barracks could withstand much of a stiffer wind than we were getting right then.

As was his weekend custom, the old boy was stewed to the gills, but he was still able to function. Anyhow, he didn't say very much but he did listen to me and he was looking the situation over. He did say that he didn't believe that it would amount to anything. However, he did tell me to just hold on and he'd be back later and let us know whether to make any move.

I went back inside to my room, lay down on my bunk, and tried to snooze. No luck there. The wind by this time was so strong that there was no doubt in anyone's mind as to whether our barracks were being shaken.

In a little while I noticed that water was beginning to cover the ground. Now that shook me up a right smart. I just stuck by the window so I could watch for the major's car. It didn't come. In fact, it never did. I thought he might have gone back home and to bed.

When this thought occurred to me, I really began getting nervous. When I noticed the water again, well, I thought I could actually see it rising. There was no question about the wind's getting stronger all the time, and the rain was steady and hard.

I continued my vigil for the major.

I don't remember at just what point I began to seriously consider my having to assume the responsibility of getting my men out of there on my own hook—without any permission or orders from anyone else. It's safe to say, though, that somewhere along the line I began thinking it over. After all, the major didn't say HOW LONG it would be before he would be back to give any of us the word.

The water was all over everywhere and rapidly getting deeper. I was doing some heavy worrying about getting out of that old trap of a building. You see, I sure didn't want anything happening to yours truly. Nobody had told me I just had to stay right there. I guess you could say that there had been an implied order to stay put when the major had told me to hold everything and he'd be back.

All manner of thoughts were flying through my feeble mind, but the one that hung in there the hardest was that of 56 recruits who certainly were not likely to make any move without someone's telling them something.

With the increasing intensity of that storm it dawned on me that I had better think up some contingency plan of getting me and those men out of there back to safer territory, just in case the major COULDN'T or didn't get back.

There was a knock on my door, and I invited the knocker to "Come in." Three recruits walked in and the biggest one of em asked me if I had ever seen or been in a hurricane. That fellow's name was Sidney J. Chastain.

I told em that I had. Then Chastain told me that all the recruits were scared that our barracks wouldn't stand up.

Another quick look out the window for the major who didn't show up.

Then I turned to Chastain and told him to get the men down from upstairs. As soon as they were all there, I told them that they were going to leave that place. Told them to take nothing but their rifles and to be sure they were floating in oil. Also that they were to wear their cartridge belts.

When they got back downstairs, ready to go, I told them that we would go out single file with the biggest men up front down to the shortest and that I'd bring up the rear. Also told them that they were to hold onto the man in front by his belt and get a death grip on it. Then I warned that if any man felt the hold on his belt turn loose that I wanted him to turn and grab his man. Those who were behind were also told to get their man back in that line. They all indicated that they understood. They slung their rifles and we started out. The water by this time was more than knee deep.

I stood out in the yard at the steps to see that all made it out. Just as the very last man's feet left the porch, our barracks just seemed to have been struck by a giant hammer. It was flattened and most of it gone. I grabbed hold of the last man's belt and we headed for the main station.

Only once did a man lose his hold on the man's belt in front of him, and the instant he did two men grabbed for him and we made it to the new brick barracks without further incident.

Before we made it, however, I asked myself a million times, "Why did you have these men bring those rifles?" And, of course, if I'd had to do it over, I most assuredly wouldn't have. Most of those rifles had to be surveyed (turned in) because of salt water damage. The bores were pitted. No doubt, subconsciously, I remembered how, as a recruit, it had been drilled into me to hold on to my rifle—regardless. And, besides, the rifle was the most valuable possession of each man.

It was late that night before we got any chow, and I was worried a right smart about where my men and I would sleep that night.

And then there were consequences.

AFTER THE HURRICANE

It was mid-afternoon of the next day after the hurricane when I got word to report to Col. Jones's office. I had been mighty busy all morning getting my platoon re-outfitted after we had gone back to where our old barracks had been to see if there was anything that we could salvage. There was nothing. We could see articles of clothing and some blankets and sheets lodged in nearby trees. We left them there.

I had sort of halfway expected to get called into somebody's office. I thought it might be the Major's office, the Training Officer who had failed to return the day before to let us know what he wanted us to do. I thought Colonel Jones might send for me. Actually, I was hoping that if I got called into anybody's office that it would be no one's but, maybe, the First Sergeant's.

I got down to Col. Jones's office as fast as I could. When I reported to the first sergeant and told him the Colonel had sent for me, that was as far as I got. Ordinarily he would have gone into the Colonel's office and told him that I was there. He didn't have time to do that. Col. Jones came and met me. He told me to come on into his office. I followed him in and stood rigidly at attention in front of his desk.

He went around and sat down behind his desk, and then he looked up at me and without taking his long black cigar out of his mouth, he said, "Bagley, you disobeyed a direct order yesterday. Did you know that?" "Yes, Sir."

Now I'm here to tell you that I had a lot of things in mind that I felt that should be said in my behalf. It was obvious from his opening statement that he had been in touch with Major Farron. And, I

thought that, even so, the fact could hardly be overlooked that had I not acted exactly when I did that it was very possible that 56 recruits would have lost their lives and also I might have been another fatality.

But I kept my thoughts to myself and simply answered, "Yes, Sir."

He didn't keep me in suspense but a moment. After my quiet admission to his charge of disobeying a direct order, he grabbed his long cigar from his mouth and came from behind his desk and took my right hand gave it a powerful shaking. Then he put his arm around my shoulders and began saying a mighty lot of nice things to me. He was, he said, very proud of me for having saved the lives of 57 men—which meant that he was including ME.

He went on. And on. And on. During his long talkathon he informed me that I had done exactly the right thing. He said, and he was referring to the Major, "In the absence of higher authority, you were in command; you were in charge."

When he paused long enough to give me an opportunity to say anything, I had to tell him, "Sir, I wasn't thinking just of the recruits alone. I was also thinking of saving my own hide."

This didn't phase the old boy. He was strung out in doing some fine bragging on me. That was all something I was not accustomed to hearing, and I didn't quite know how to take it.

He mentioned about some kind of medal. Then he went on to say, "Now if this had happened in war time . . . " I figured that right there went the chance of any kind of medal. I don't really know just where all my thoughts were other than that I was receiving some kind of commendation just by standing there and listening to him say what he was saying.

It seemed that he just couldn't say enough. He asked me how it felt to realize that those 56 men owed their lives to me. I had to tell him, "Sir, I'm just real happy that we all got out of there alive and nobody got hurt."

When he digested this and made a remark about my deed being one of heroics, and a few other things, I felt that it was safe for me to tell him that even though I had already made up my mind to move my men, I had not decided to do it at just the time I did—not until the three recruits came to my room asking if I'd ever been in a hurricane. As I told him, "That was the time I decided to do it RIGHT

THEN." I had to go on and tell him that the recruits themselves had given me the last little push that I needed to move.

Now when the Colonel was making all this chit chat about a medal, the thought that kept running through my mind was that he could very easily have given me a promotion from corporal to sergeant, or even two extra stripes and made me a platoon sergeant. That would have meant more money each month. But not once did the old boy mention anything about any promotion. Not a word.

The next thing he began talking about was that since he couldn't do this medal job that he would have me stand in the reviewing stand at the very next parade. I put in a mild protest. Mild but sincere. I was telling him the honest to goodness truth when I told him that if it was all the same to him we'd just skip that bit about the parade.

He sternly informed me that I would be on the parade ground the following Thursday afternoon at 1500 (3 P.M.) and that I had better be in the reviewing stand. I said, "Yes, Sir." As he dismissed me, he told me to wear my dress blues because the parade would be held in my honor.

I did. It was. And he so informed the troops when they were all lined up and just before they passed in review.

In about a couple of weeks I began getting a load of mail. It came from parents, girl friends, grandparents. It was obvious that my boys had written home and they must have painted an entirely new picture of me than the one they had been sending along to their loves ones. I kept all those letters for years and I had intended to hang onto them forever, but in all the moves I've made since that time, somehow, somewhere, they got left behind. And right now I'd give my eye teeth for them; even just ONE of them!

Speaking of the medal, or of a promotion the Colonel didn't mention, I have often thought of that day and what followed: If he had done anything other than what he did, I imagine that somehow it would have had to be noted that the Training Officer had sorta neglected his duty that terrible Sunday.

Anyhow, I noticed that not once did the Colonel mention the Major's name. You can bet that I didn't either.

I do want you to know that I derived a mighty great pleasure and got so much satisfaction from those letters I received from the families of my men. And I would be remiss if I did not tell you that each of them thanked me personally before they left the Island. After those men shipped out a few weeks later, I went back to my bunk in my room to lie down and relax for a little while.

As soon as I saw my bunk I spotted a big hump under the pillow so I immediately investigated. There was a big wad of newspaper rolled up and I found inside that $300. Maybe I should have taken the money and turned it in to the first sergeant, but . . . Ah, you can bet your bottom nickel that that went in my pocket and I kept my mouth shut. In amongst all of that tremendous amount of doogaloo was a mighty fine ''Thank you'' note signed by each of the 56 men in that HURRICANE PLATOON.

CUZ MAY TURN
TO WIDOW WATCHING

I have a good friend in Brevard, N.C. by the name of Wild Bill Williamson, and I think he has about the most interesting hobby I ever heard of. Now when I said he was a good friend, I didn't mean that he was the kind of good friend from whom I could borrow money. Actually I have never met him face to face, but we have written to each other a few times.

This correspondence between us began as a result of his hobby which I thought was kinda unusual and real interesting. Wild Bill frequently writes letters to the editor of The Asheville Citizen and they are published in the Back Talk column on the editorial page. In the letters he often spoke of his hobby and when I tell you what it is you will understand why I was so keenly interested.

I reckon you know and agree that everybody should have a hobby. Hobbies are good for taking up spare time and keeping you out of mischief. Every once in a while we read about people who get so good with their hobbies that they turn them into full time occupations and earn their bread and butter with them. Of course, when this happens then they have to turn to something else for a hobby.

I read just the other day about a man over around Franklin, N.C. who began potting some flowers as a hobby. Before he got through with it, darned if he didn't just go into the flower potting business complete. But I guess it was a lot better for him to get all those flowers potted instead of himself. Probably he will turn to fishing now as his hobby. Who knows, maybe then he would become a a commercial fisherman and then he could go back to potting flowers as a hobby.

Wild Bill's hobby is a lot better than potting flowers or anything like that on account of it does not resemble work in any respect. Right there is another reason it seems so interesting to me. I have always been opposed to any kind of pastime which involved any physical exercise. My friend's hobby seems to require the very minimum of that as he says it isn't necessary to lug any equipment or anything like that around with you when you are engaging in this sport—I mean hobby!

Widow watching is his hobby!!! There are a few things to keep in mind, Wild Bill advises. Keeping your distance seems to be the most important one thing to remember. He said, "The main thing to watch is—not to get too close to them. They have tricks to catch a man and will use them at the drop of a hanky. Especially those Florida Gals who hobble up here every summer, prime and primp themselves, paint and pamper their faces, discard their crutches and canes, and engage in a manhunt fast and furious."

Of course, I wouldn't have to worry any about this distance factor. If any of those watched widows appeared to be getting too close, all I'd have to do would be take off my hat and my peeled onion head would be enough to scare them off. If that failed I'd try to think of something else.

My B. W. has already taken note of my interest in Wild Bill's hobby. I don't think she paid too much attention to this interchange of letters between us, though, until the night of the Miss Universe Pageant. I'll tell you what put her to thinking. When they narrowed the contestants down to the 15 semi-finalists and paraded these gals, one by one, before the cameras, I spotted Miss Greece (I bet not a one of you could spell her name any better than I could) and I tagged her as the winner of that shindig.

My B. W. and my daughter both made all kinds of fun of me for picking her. They both chose the gal from England. When they cut the 15 down to the 10 finalists, my pick was still in there. Then they began announcing the runners-up. Miss Greece was not among em naturally, so B. W. and Sharon said, "See, she is not even gonna be a runner-up." You doggoned right she wasn't cause she had just won all the marbles and they were saving her to announce last. All of which goes to prove that Ole Cuz sure knows how to pick out a purty gal.

Before the pageant officials managed to get that crown to stay on the top of that beautiful dame's head, my B. W. said mightly solemnly, "You better not let me catch you doing any widow watching." And just as solemnly, I promised her that I'd do my dead-level best to see that she didn't catch me at it.

THE IMMIGRANT

"Boats" was a man's man—big but humble, proud but not arrogant, rough but understanding, eager to talk but willing to listen, strong as a bull but kind in his own way.

He had character. He was honest. He had principle. He had seen and experienced the seamy side of life—raw, rough, ridiculed, rejected, and rebellious in nature. He had also seen the wholesome side of life—repented, renewed, redeemed, and reconciled with God.

He had determination.

Born in Germany in 1897—lived to be 70 years old. A ship's hand in his early teens. He was in Chile when World War I broke out. He came to the United States in 1916. He served in the U.S. Army from 1923 till 1927 and in the Coast Guard from 1943 till 1945. He became a U.S. Citizen in 1942, and he loved his adopted homeland in a way that should be an example and an inspiration to us nativeborn. He wrote some prose one time about "Democracy" in which he said, "You give democracy life by living it, for living it you will understand it, understanding it you will love it; and loving it you will want to live in no other way."

He had conviction.

He had been a Methodist. He was a Baptist at the time of his death. Most of all, he was a Christian. He knew God and he knew Christ, his Lord. He wrote a poem, "Created in Thy Image, Lord?" and in it he said, "Lord of land, of air, of sea//Master of all there is, of all there is to be//Thou art the Creator of all, Lord . . . Thy Son was sent to save me//Created in Thy image, Lord? As I would ask, wouldst Thou then answer me? As I am now? As I have been? As I will always be? How can, how could my image ever be like thee?"

He knew the majesty of God.
He knew the lowliness of man.
And in between he knew the redemption Christ provides.

A poet, philosopher, prophet, political analyst, and a personal friend.

The Lord is his shepherd now; he does not want. His shepherd has seen him through the valley of the shadow of death. And he continues to read, to meditate, to write, to argue, to discuss, and to grow.

He had seen through a glass darkly, but now he sees face to face.

He wrote a poem once entitled, "Prayer," with these words in it:

"As it is in Heaven, so on earth Thy will shall be and yet, against Thy mighty, holy will I wish my foolish wish; so foolishly grant me, My Lord, I ask it in His name, that Thy will and my wish may some day be the same." Today God's will and his wish are the same.

The Rev. Mr. Robert T. Young, Minister of the Skyland, N.C. Methodist Church made the above tribute to my friend, Boats Schoeler, and I thought it should be shared with you.

Of course it would have been necessary to have known my friend to have been able to fully appreciate his many unusual and admirable qualities.

Bob Young said he had determination. He had it in abundance! Enough so that after each of many, many major operations he always bounced back with, seemingly, as much fierce determination as ever to conquer each new physical handicap.

His long siege of troubles began when he was wounded in WW II and ended on May 27 when he finally had to surrender.

Any time I ever visited Boats he would endeavor to minimize his own difficulties. He was always far more concerned about my ailments! And around him I actually was ashamed ever to admit that I had had a single ache or pain. Any time!

"To Tom," penned by Boats, was adopted by the Thomas Wolfe Memorial Association and now hangs in Wolfe's old homeplace in Asheville, N.C.

To Tom

You were the ghostly haunter of yourself, forever haunted
By the lost, the part remembered, part forgotten memory
That if but found and all remembered or but all forgotten

Would then have eased your tortured soul and made you free.
But you became the curious stranger in life's noisy inn
And sailed the dark, forbidden sea that until then had
    never seen a sail.
The argonauts of yore, the ancient, the titanic heroes were your kin.
In this, your epic search for golden fleece and holy grail
You've lit the torch, you proved that darkness must and can be overcome;
So now your work, your search will never cease
For all will carry on that really understand, know this, Oh Tom,
And rest you now, for once, in peace.

                                      Ernest Schoeler
                                      Skyland, N.C.

HAPPINESS, BIRDS & JACOB

I don't have a thing against happiness. For people. But I am dead set against it for birds and I'll tell you why. I had a wonderful idea for a great column. Funny as it could be. And as I lay in bed trying to get it all together in my feeble mind, suddenly some very happy whippoorwill began to sing to me. Now you may be able to think sensibly and all, regardless of all kinds of racket going on right under your nose. But not me. I have to have peace and quiet to do almost any kind of thinking.

They kept the noise going until I forgot all about what I had originally planned to write about. During the course of their bellering, though, I did seriously consider, first, shooting a .22 rifle out in the general direction of their happiness. But I ruled this out as I didn't think it would make a loud enough bang to scare them off toward Cliff Henry's. And, besides, Cliff is such a fine neighbor and friend that my conscience would not allow me to wish anything like that off on him.

However, after about two solid hours of this pestification I began considering getting up and shooting a shotgun out at these happy birds. I had to rule this out also as this shotgun is one I have borrowed from Cliff and if he heard it blast out in the middle of the night . . . well, he just might get up and come to my house and want it back. Right then.

So I gave up on attempting to think bout that particular column. I thought I would get up bright and early the next morning to finish thinking it up and writing it.

Know what happened a little BEFORE bright and early that next morning? More happy birds began singing right in my ears. Anyhow you can just forget about that real funny column. I already have. And that's why I'm having to borrow something—steal is really the word I should use for what I'll be writing about.

Before I get started on it, though, I just want to make this comment. All this racket I'm having to put up with at my house is on account of daylight saving time that our lawmakers voted in for the summer months. Why, it is too! You just think back to the winter months when we were on regular time. You just don't hear any happy birds hollering late at night or early in the morning. No, they go to bed at a sensible hour and they don't get up until way after daylight. In the wintertime.

I got the following from our Truett Baptist Association's "Baptist Recorder." They copied it from somebody else but they didn't say from who. Or it is whom? Anyhow, here it is:

"HOW MUCH DO YOUR PUPILS REALLY KNOW ABOUT WHAT GOD'S WORD SAYS? WOULD YOU PASS THIS TEST." A preacher entered a class while the lesson was in progress and asked this question, "Who broke down the walls of Jericho?" A boy answered, "Not me, sir." The preacher turned to the teacher and asked, "Is this the usual behavior of this class?" The teacher answered, "This boy is honest and I believe him. I really don't think he did it."

Leaving the room the preacher sought an elder and explained what had happened. The elder said, "I have known both the teacher and the boy for years, and neither of them would do such a thing."

By this time the preacher was heartsick and reported it to the Department of Christian Education. They said, "We see no point in being disturbed. Let's pay the bill for the damage to the walls and charge it to upkeep."

I am happy to report to you that I did not flunk that test. And in case you don't remember who broke down those walls of Jericho, I'll tell you. It sure wasn't ME, either. Actually it was Jacob. I know you remember about Jacob and his ladder. Well, if you want to look it up in the Bible it is on page 532. You remember that Jacob was climbing his ladder one night and he was in a big hurry, didn't have the ladder set just right, it slipped and fell, breaking down the walls of Jericho and one of the flying rocks from that wall hit some unidentified fellow up side the head and he and Jacob fit a knock-down drag-out fight all night long and pore ole Jacob wound up with a bruised hip.

As I recollect it Jacob got that bruised hip in all this fighting. I reckon he wasn't too high up on his ladder or he'd have gotten all busted up when he fell.

Now if you happen to be a Sunday School teacher you will probably want to read this to your next class so you can have your youngans well informed on this matter of who broke down those walls.

A DRY EYED FUNERAL

This is about one of them dry-eyed funerals.

You have probably been to some of these kinda funerals too, I'll bet. You know where nobody does any crying a tall. These are the worst kind to go to. And I would never attend one of these if I had my way about it. Would you? I had a lot rather go to them where everybody cries and hollers and has a good time.

I never will forget going to one of these dry-eyed ones one time. It was just the worst one that I was ever at. The fellow that was dead was an ole reprobate, an ole ne'er-do-well, and a real genuine stinker. And everybody in the community said that if he ever did die, you see we all figured he was too mean to die, but he finally did anyhow—well, we all thought there wouldn't be enough folks that would care to be able to find six men to tote him to his hole. In fact, he was so mean and ornery that we doubted anybody would even dig him one.

When he finally did kick off, some of the folks did dig one for him and they got six fellows that promised to tote him to his hole, but only because they were anxious to see that he was in one.

I never knew preachers could be so busy as everyone in the whole country seemed to be when word got out that ole Sefe had died. Finally they found a young preacher that had not heard of ole Sefe and he agreed to come and preach over him.

And he did. News got out that this young preacher was gonna do the preaching and there was a pretty good turn out after all. Even some of them "busy preachers" came to hear him. It amounted to a kind of Trial Sermon for this young preacher.

Well, he got started off sorta nervously. He was anxious to make a good impression as he was new at this business and kinda looking around for him a church. He said a real good prayer. He was pleading with the Lord about comforting the hearts of the bereaved. He prayed this matter over a right smart longer than it took anybody to get over their bereavement. Then he led a song, "Nearer My God To Thee," but we all knew that this young preacher was confused about the direction ole Sefe was headed. After that song he looked the congregation over to see if anybody had started crying. Nobody had, so then he led "Shall We Gather at the River." Still no tears. So he started preaching. And he preached and preached. I belive he must have thought that unless he could preach em to tears he wasn't doing no good a tall. And it looked like he meant to keep on until he got somebody to squalling.

My Aunt Lula realized this too, so she set in to weeping and wailing. And I might say right here that she was mighty good at it too. In fact you just couldn't hardly have a funeral nowhere in the community without Aunt Lula. She was such a good weeper and wailer. Usually she could get everybody started. I guess you could say that she led the weeping and wailing like the song leader does the singing. Anyhow she was taking on so that this young preacher finally hushed and asked if someone wouldn't please go and comfort the "poor sister." Nobody made a move cause we all knew that she was just putting on. Finally Papa got up and came over to her and whispered in her ear loud enough for her to hear, as well as several others that were sitting in her vicinity, "Shut yore mouth." Then he patted her on the shoulder a time or two and went on back to his seat. Aunt Lula raised her head up, dabbed her eyes that were as dry as my pocket, blowed her nose, punched me in the side with her elbow, and took a song book out of the rack. Then I had to hide my face, not because I was squalling though. It took nearly all I could do to keep from laughing out loud at Papa and Aunt Lula.

Along about here the preacher must have realized that something was haywire cause he hushed in another minute or two, and they took ole Sefe on out and buried him.

A PLACE FOR EVERYTHING

I won't ever forget how Mama used to fuss at us youngans about keeping our stuff picked up. She's say, "A place for everything and everything in its place." Mama had a lot of sayings that she'd quote to us. However, I believe this was the one I heard most often.

And it did seem to me that I got "picked on the most." Actually she wasn't doing anything of the kind. She merely liked to see the house, occasionally anyhow, look something less than like a tornado had struck it. And my room was always (mine and Ray's, when he got big enough to sleep with me), according to her, in the worst mess.

Now when you were growing up, maybe your folks had a maid to clean house, make beds, cook and wash dishes, wash windows, and all the other menial and disagreeable tasks that, particularly, mamas can find around the house. But we didn't. From the time we were big enough for anything Mama found things for us to do.

About the first instructions I can remember getting were on how to make my bed. Mama showed and told me, showed and told me, showed and told me, and if she did once, I'll betcha she must've done so thousands of times. I just never heard of anybody who was so particular.

Soon after the bed-making instructions, and perhaps even before, she began talking about "picking up my stuff," hanging up my clothes, and things like that.

Course she never insisted on my hanging anything in a closet. Reason for that was we didn't have any. Now this wasn't any inconvenience; it was a CONvenience. You see this eliminated a chore—I didn't have any closet to clean out. But I did have nails in the wall on which to hang clothes. And other things that just had to be hung up.

Wouldn't you think that with just nails to hang clothes on it'd be all right to just, maybe, throw em up there? I used to be able to wad my overalls and shirt up and throw em at this one big 60-penny nail and they'd catch on nearly every time. But, no siree, this didn't suit our Mama a tall—that is when she saw em sorta lodged on this nail.

There was a particular way, I found out, that overhalls and shirts should be hung on nails. First you buckled both galluses and hung them over the nail, and then you hung the collar of the shirt over nail and galluses. And woe be unto ye if you got mixed up and did it backwards. Mama said, "Always hang the shirt up last on account of you have to put it on first." That's when she'd say, "The first shall be last, and the last shall be first." Like I said, Mama had a lotta sayings.

Now the books and magazines, slingshots and rocks (for ammo), pocket knives, marbles, magnifying glass, pieces of string, arrowheads, corks, lines, and fish hooks, as well as various and sundry other necessary equipment, such as squirrel tails, rabbit feet, etc.—Well, I just had to watch Mama close or she'd lose a lot of this valuable material.

You know where? Why, she'd "put it up." And, I'll tell you when she "put it up," Mister, a lotta times that meant it was just gone. She'd say, "If you'd just learn to put things up, you'd know where they were."

Time and time again I did my dead level best to convince her that if I managed to get in my room with it that, as far as I was concerned, it WAS PUT UP. She had decidedly different ideas about that.

A few times I even tried to persuade her to just kinda ignore my room, shut the door and forget about it. But I never pursued the subject too persistently on account of Mama's patience had its limits.

But I used to look forward to the time I could have my very own house. Then, I'd say to myself, I'll leave things exactly where I want to and nobody, but NOBODY, would EVER make me put it up, pick it up, or hang it up.

Well, I lived to realize my ambition of having my very own—I mean OUR very own house. And that "OUR" business is what made all the difference. If I made you think that Mama made a big to-do over this, a place for everything, etc. business, then let me clear that up. She wasn't fussy a tall. No Siree. What she did was she eventually just gave up, on me that is.

And you'd think that a woman'd give up out of sheer frustration after having lived under the same roof with somebody like me as long as my B. W. has, but she sure hasn't. All these years her spirits have never flagged, her determination has been firm and resolute, and I reckon she must figure that, if the two of us live long enough, some day she'll get me in the habit of keeping everything nice, neat and orderly.

* * *

"If you're looking for sympathy you can find it in the dictionary between shoot and suicide."

- Attributed to a U. S. Marine Corps Drill Instructor.

THANKSGIVING CORDIAL

Papa used to make up some stuff he called Thanksgiving Cordial. But I found out later that it really wasn't anything but just plain wine. And he sure didn't believe in being caught short of plenty of cordial at Thanksgiving time, and at Christmas, the Fourth of July, Washington's Birthday, as well as Abe Lincoln's, and especially Jefferson Davis's, and Robert E. Lee's. Tell you the truth, I just never knew Papa to be short of some kind of cordial, I don't care who had a birthday or something like that.

It might be well to say right along here that I never knew there were so many occasions that just couldn't hardly take place a tall without a little cordial to go along with em—even weekends and Mondays.

Now there were just certain things, special kinds of fruit, that would do to make cordial out of. Let's see. Papa used scuppernongs; these made a powerful good cordial. Then strawberries, and I sure liked the cordiality that they seemed to be full of, especially before they got all through bubbling and spewing and fizzing off. Papa called this process a ferment. Blackberries did pretty well too, if you handled em right, and my Papa always understood just exactly how anything like this oughta be handled.

We also grew a lot of figs and had a sight of em left over after Mama made all the preserves she could find jars for. And Papa sure didn't believe in leaving bushels of these on the trees for the jay birds and mockingbirds, so we picked em and, according to Papa, to keep them from going to waste—he just didn't believe in anything being let go to waste. Yes, we picked em and Papa made Thanksgiving Cordial out of em. Extry good too.

And you might not think you could make anything like what Papa did outta tomatoes. But now when we had a lotta them left over, that's right, they got cordialed up just like the scuppernongs, blackberries and everything else on the place.

Why, one time I remember he even decided that we had a whole bunch of Irish potatoes that were sure to go bad unless he hurried up to make something out of them. He told me that he thought potatoes were what the Rooshuns made some kinda cordial out of.

Papa always seemed like he was mighty sorry for the "Rooshuns" on account of potatoes was all he ever heard of that they knew how to make into any cordial. He said there wasn't much wonder that they all seemed to be such a sour bunch of folks.

Now outta apples, Papa always made vinegar cause a certain amount of it was necessary for Mama's peach and cucumber pickles. Then too she had to dry a lot of em for tarts and pies in the winter. Of course if any of em happened to get left over Papa had already figured how they too could be kept from going to waste.

And peaches! There was just no such thing as being able to preserve, pickle, and dry all of them. So out of those Papa'd fix up some stuff that he didn't call Cordial; it was brandy. But he said it could be used just like you did Thanksgiving Cordial. And he was right.

Mama used to give Papa down the country every once in a while because she said that it looked like to her that he was a lot more interested in making up Cordial than he was getting stuff fixed up in any other way. But he argued that it was also mighty important to have fruit an' stuff preserved in more ways than one or two. And, "Besides," he said, "What would family reunions and gatherings such as that be like if you was to run out of Cordial?"

Mama said many a time that she sure would like to see what one of those reunions would be if there wasn't a drop of none of that stuff to lubricate em with. Papa'd just kinda chuckle when Mama'd get strung out on him about his ample stock of wine—I mean Cordial. It used to tickle me to hear em get into it about that stuff. I could tell Papa wasn't making any plans a tall for coming up with any shortages in his department.

Now I sure wouldn't have you think that my Papa was any ole sot cause he sure wasn't. Actually he was a powerful man with the Scriptures, and he didn't hold one bit with anybody having too much O Be Joyful. Sure nuff, he could prove near bout anything with the

Scriptures. For instance, any time he and Mama'd get into it 'bout all the Cordial he made he would always remind her about what that fellow Paul told Timothy; you know, about a little wine for the stomach's sake.

Of course she knew the Scriptures too, and she'd quote him some also that seemed to be about as strong against the stuff as his was for it. But Papa allowed that he reckoned that part about a "little wine for the stomach's sake" was just about the strongest Scripture there was in the whole Bible. That's the way Papa was; if he believed anything a tall, he said he just couldn't see no sense in it if a body didn't believe in it good and strong.

VICTIM OF CIRCUMSTANCES

There was just no other way to look at it. I was a victim of circumstances. Mama didn't see it that way, but we often differed in our way of looking at a lot of things.

It was the spring of 1927 when Mama and I had this particular difference of opinion. Of course, we also had other disagreements that same year, but this one was, by far, the most notable. It sure was as far as I was concerned.

We were living in Brewton, Alabama at the time. Actually it was East Brewton. It was already becoming fashionable to designate different sections of a city or town with East so and so, or North this or that. This town was kinda small, though, and all it had was the Brewton part and the East Brewton part. The city fathers soon realized that if they cut the town up any more there wouldn't be any Brewton left.

There were some thriving businesses in our town then. Like the T. R. Miller Mill Co., Luttrell's Hardware (This is where I bought BB's for my air rifle.) and Hutto's. I'll always remember Hutto's cause in front of that store was a sign with a hut painted on it and then some toes beside it. Everybody knew where Hutto's was.

Then, Harvey's Barber Shop. I liked to get my hair cut there cause you could watch the trains longer as they rolled through the middle of town. This sometimes made Mr. Harvey's job of cutting my hair kinda rough. However, he was quick to catch on and soon learned to turn his chair so I could watch the train out of sight. Occasionally he would just quit altogether and we would both count the cars as they went by. I soon learned he was a better barber than he was a car counter.

Then there was Robin's & McGowan's. The way this was pronounced was Robgowans. It was an industrious little city. Why, I'll tell you it was the richest town for its size of nearly 'bout anywhere. It was the wealthiest town in Escambia County. I'll tell you something else too. There wasn't but one Courthouse in the county and Brewton had it.

In 1927 we had a flood. Ole Noah thought he had a flood. He should have seen ours. Besides all the raining it did around there a big dam busted up north of us, and I sure don't remember reading about any dams getting busted nowhere to help Noah out with his flood.

This was the best flood I ever saw. There was only one thing wrong with it. It didn't get no more than knee deep around the school house. Even though it had that one shortcoming of not having washed the school house away, it was an extra good flood on account of we didn't have to go to school for a couple of weeks. That allowed me, Jake, Ed Neal Scott, Claudis Beasley, Tommy Whittington, and Potlicker Capps to catch up with a lot of important things we were behind with.

When the water began going down, people went back to their homes, if they were still there, to clean up. Steve Barnes was fixing to go check on his place. He had found a small boat and just before shoving off he asked us boys if we would like to go along. All of em cept me were pretty sure their mamas wouldn't want em to be gone all day. Since I wasn't all that sure I decided I'd better go along with him to see if his house was still there. Anyhow I wouldn't have had time before Steve left to go back home and ask Mama whether she cared if I went.

It was one of those times when I had to make a decision in a hurry. And it was obvious that any delay would surely cause me to miss the boat. Steve wanted to know if my folks knew where I was. I assured him they did, and also that Mama wouldn't care one bit if I was gone awhile. This was a slight error in judgment.

Actually it was just a big lie.

We paddled off down the road about two miles past Cedar Hill and finally reached Steve's house in time to eat. The water was already down to about knee deep so we waded into his house to fix our grub. He let me climb up in the attic where he had put his chickens and gather the eggs. While I was up there I caught the chickens and turned them loose. They were all easy caught except that ole Dominecker rooster. Before coming down I handed Steve some planks that he used to make a fire in the stove. Those were the best scrambled eggs I ever ate.

We did what cleaning up we could and headed back about the middle of the afternoon. The water was soon too shallow to paddle the boat, so we waded the rest of the way back.

When I got home there was a lot of neighbor women there at the house. They were trying to comfort Mama, who was sure I had been swallowed up in that flood.

As soon as Virginia saw me she ran and told Mama who came and nearly bout hugged me in two, and kissed me right there in front of everybody. She just cried, then laughed, then cried some more. But this didn't last long. Before she hardly got through hugging me, she had Papa's razor strap. And she didn't sharpen his razor with it either. When she first got her hands on me I sorta thought it was just like the story I had heard about in Sunday School about the prodigal son's return. There the similarity ended. I could never convince Mama that I hadn't been a victim of circumstances. She said she was SURPRISED at me. I don't think she really was but she did say so.

GRANDPA, LIKKER & PREACHERS

My great-grandpa was a corker, so I've been told. I never knew him cause he had already passed on before I arrived on the scene.

When I said that about his being a corker maybe you thought I meant he was some kinda character, but he wasn't. What I meant was that he did a lot of corking and uncorking. You see, he liked a little nip occasionally. So, every time he wanted this nip he'd have to uncork his jug, then recork it.

I was told that he didn't actually use any cork, what he used for the stopper was a corn cob which served the same purpose. Corncobs were surely handy on the farm. I reckon he could also have been called an ole Cobber but I never heard of one of them and I don't think Noah Webster ever did either. However, I have heard of, and know a few, corkers. Webster did too.

Papa used to tell me a lot about Grandpa Dred Bagley. The story about his being a corker, I guess, was the one I enjoyed hearing the most.

I mentioned about his liking an occasional nip. It would have been far more accurate to have said he liked it regularly cause, according to Papa, that's how he had it. It seemed that every morning as soon as he woke up he'd sit on the side of the bed, then reach under there and get his jug, uncork it, and have himself a pretty good slug of homemade corn likker. Back then everybody made their own. These were the days before the bootlegger, also before Prohibition.

Papa said this nipping also came before each meal, and now and then he might sorta need pepping up in the middle of the morning, and maybe in the afternoons. He said he and his brothers used to really enjoy staying with Grandpa Dred cause he'd always send one of them for his jug when he felt the need of a little swaller. Naturally they got to sampling the stuff and Papa said it was powerful strong medicine. Several times he said they got a leetle too much, but it never made em sick. Only made em that much gladder they'd come to stay with Grandpa.

Now I'd not have you thinking my Great-Grandpa was an ole sot cause he sure wasn't. In fact, it was said of the old gentleman that he didn't hold with overdoing it. He was a church going man and according to Papa, Grandpa had been instrumental in "Churching" more than one for making public spectacles of themselves when they over-tilted the jug, or maybe beat their wives up more'n common.

The story was that one preacher sorta took the old man to task, in other words, gave him down the country about this nipping business. That's when Grandpa reminded this preacher that on page 735 in the Bible it told about what St. Paul said to Timothy on the subject. And that was a little wine would be good for what ailed him. Grandpa sure knew the Bible. But this preacher was very determined and told the old man that fooling with the demon rum would get the best of him. It turn out the preacher was right, as they frequently are, and it sure did get the best of Ole Grandpa, at the age of ninety-seven.

A friend of mine told me this story. A young lady remarked that she wanted to marry either a doctor, so she could stay well for nothing, or a preacher so she could stay good for nothing.

I guess I am already in pretty bad with preachers so I guess I might as well tell you another one or two on em. You know I don't understand why they should object to stories about themselves—they sure don't mind peeling the bark on all of us. You know how they are. All you have to do is show em a pulpit and they begin waxing eloquent about us ole sinners.

Three old maid sisters died and went to heaven. St. Peter interviewed them on their arrival. Each was asked how many sins she had committed on earth. Number One declared she had only slipped up 3 times. She was awarded a Cadillac to ride around in up there. Number Two admitted she had sinned 25 times. She got a motor scooter. Number Three frankly declared that she had no idea how many sins were charged to her account. She got a bicycle. Shortly after they had been to the supply rooms to claim their respective vehicles sisters One and Two heard Three almost laughing her wings off. They located her and asked how come. She said, "I just saw our preacher go sailing by here on a pair of roller skates."

A fire and brimstone preacher was the visiting evangelist in a small country church. When he and the regular pastor walked down to the pulpit they found an old hound sleeping peacefully. The V. P. hauled off and gave old Rover a good swift kick, you know to sorta illustrate how he was gonna handle old Satan when he got all limbered up. Rover left just a-yelping. The pastor of the church said, "Brother, I'm sure sorry you done that, on account of that hound you just kicked belongs to the chairman of my board of deacons."

After the service the V. P. hunted up this deacon and began apologizing for his unseemly conduct. The deacon said, "Why, Parson, don't you worry one bit about it cause you done me a favor." The V. P. asked, "How's that?" And the deacon told him, "Cause that's the best hound I ever owned and I wouldn't have had him hear that sermon you just preached for $325.00."

"PAPA NEAL"

Papa Neal loved to go places. He really liked that riding around, and he knew that when we came home, to Andalusia, Alabama, that he would get to do a heap o' going on account of every time we made that trip down home I would go see all my kinfolks and old friends. And he knew them all, and he also knew that I would take him with me. He knew those who were scalawags and of course he knew the few of my relatives who made decent citizens. Believe it or not, but some of em did. Maybe there were more of the other kind but I enjoyed hearing about them all. Why he even knew my great grandfather Dred Bagley.

While catching our breath, between trips, one day, we were sitting on the front gallery in the swing. Suddenly Papa Neal got real quiet and seemed to be considering something very seriously. Then he said, "Harry, I want you to do something for me." Now without a moment's hesitation I answered, "You name it and I'll do it." I thought that he had remembered someone or some place that he wanted me to take him to see.

I certainly wasn't prepared for what he said next. He said, "Good. I'm 84 years old and I know that I couldn't have much longer to stay here, so when I pass on I want you to perform my Masonic burial service." Well, I want you to know that I almost fell out of that swing! And talk about trying to get off the hook, I mean to tell you that I began giving him a passel of reasons why I couldn't do a thing like THAT! My own father-in-law!! I had been a member of the fraternity for only about four months and doing a Masonic burial service was the last thing, well, I'd just never even given the matter a thought.

None of my protests did a bit of good. He kept reminding me that I had promised him that I'd do whatever it was he wanted.

Finally, I said, "Why, Papa, I might not even have time to learn it before it would need to be done. He had a ready answer. "I'm going to do my best to give you plenty of time."

So when I got back home, I began working on it. When I finally had it memorized I wrote and told him, "All right, Sir, now I'm ready when you are." An immediate reply came back. He said, "Young man, let's not be in any hurry about this thing."

The dreaded day eventually came, and I fulfilled his wishes but I can assure you that that task was the very most difficult one I had ever attempted. Somehow I got through it without a bobble. It was afterward that I came apart at the seams.

Papa used to love to play cards and checkers. I didn't play him but very few games of checkers on account of I couldn't hold him a light, and in no time at all he wouldn't even mention the game because he would just slap tear me up every time. And he wanted some competition which I was never able to give him. So that took care of checkers. He liked set-back and poker for his card games. But I knew better than to even start any poker game with him. We played partners in set-back against Mama Neal and my BW. If we lost, which we did most of the time, Papa would give me down the country for not playing it right. He'd be over it by the next morning and we'd start out on our rounds seeing kinfolks and friends.

One summer when Mary and Bob were visiting down home, they had a red hot poker game going out under the pear tree. Papa managed to get a few dollars ahead, and he suddenly told them he had to go in the house. They sat and waited on him. And they waited. When they went in to see about him, Mama Neal told them that all she knew was that he'd grabbed his hat and left. She thought he'd gone back to their poker game. Instead he had slipped out the back way, took a short cut and headed down town and bought himself a brand new shirt with his poker winnings. You see he was a mighty smart poker player. Most poker players would have sat right there under that pear tree until they LOST their shirts. But not Papa Neal. He went and BOUGHT him one. And he wouldn't play any more poker with his daughter and son-in-law that day.

Papa Neal always kept a few tools that he used around the house occasionally. And he had a special place to keep them and he flat didn't want no little youngan messing with em. He had one little grandson, Duane, who soon learned where Papa kept his tool box and when Berry and Ruby brought Little Mister Duane over, somebody would have to watch out about him or he'd have Papa Neal's tool box out in the yard with him. Duane was about four or five when this particular thing happened.

He had managed to get that tool box and out back with it. When Papa Neal went to the back door, he spotted Duane banging a screw driver into the ground with his hammer. Papa stormed out and yelled at the pore little feller, "Now, when I go over to YOUR house you don't see ME messing with YOUR tools and I want you to just leave MINE alone."

As long as Papa was able he went to town every day except Sunday. You could count on it. He had some kind of business to attend to, groceries to buy, or he just had to go. Period. And if you sat on the front porch you could see him coming a block away. Mama Neal said that there were three things you could tell about Papa just by the way he was walking. If he hadn't heard any news or seen anybody worth talking about, he was walking slow. But if he was in a big hurry he had some hot news or he needed to go to the bathroom.

I told you he liked to ride around and go see folks. Well, we'd just bought a new car in 1956 and the first trip we made in it of any distance was down home. We got there late one night. BW knew that my plans were to get up early the next morning and head on down to Pensacola, Florida and see my Mom, sisters and brother and then come back to Andalusia and spend the rest of our time there.

When Papa Neal got up that morning he went outside and gave that new automobile a good looking at. When he came back inside he began telling Mama Neal and BW of several places he needed to go that day. He just knew good and well that he and I would ride all over the place in that spanking new vehicle. Then BW told him that I was going on down to Pensacola that morning to see my folks and that I'd be back in a day or two and then, she was sure, we would go every place that either of us could think of to go. Now THAT news was just the sorriest kinda news anybody coulda given Papa just at that "point in time." He stomped on through the kitchen and announced in a very loud voice, "Well, it just looks like I ain't gonna get to ride in that ¢3#$@*#% new car after all!"

Papa Neal was one more sight. I reckon the reason I thought so much of him was on account of he always acted as if he thought the world of me. A favorite little saying of his and Mama Neal's was: Beauty is only skin deep but ugly is to the bone. Beauty will soon fade away but ugly will hold its own.''

BLIND DATE

Customs and people change, and I reckon it's a darn good thing too on account of some of the things I had in mind sure did need changing.

I was thinking, though, that some few elements of this boy-girl business still linger with us. For instance, I heard a young man talking about having a blind date all lined up for a few nights ago. And that reminded me of two of my very most memorable blind dates.

The fact that young folks still have them, blind dates I mean, is probably the only similarity still hanging on.

I'll tell you about one of those two very special B. D.'s. And later I might get around to telling about the other one. Right now I'll tell about the one that Cecil Moon got for me. The Moons were our neighbors, and Cecil and I were the best of buddies.

For some time he had been telling me that he knew two of the cutest sisters, and he wanted me to go with him some time and double date. Finally I agreed to go with him. He had everything all set up for us for one Sunday night. Actually, what I had been waiting on was a new pair of shoes. Sunday shoes.

A lot of you folks won't understand what I mean about Sunday shoes. I'll take just a jiffy here to explain that. Back then, pore folks, if they were lucky, had just two kinds of shoes: every day shoes, and Sunday shoes. The every day ones were the ones we worked in. And Sunday ones were just what the name implies. We wore these only on Sunday or other very special occasions.

When he first mentioned about these two pretty girls, I just didn't have any Sunday shoes, period. And I wasn't about to go meet any pretty new girl in my old brogans. I got my new shoes on a Saturday afternoon. And, man, did they ever smell good? Remember when you were a youngan how good a new pair of shoes used to smell? And they squeaked too. Why I wouldn't have had a new pair if they hadn't been good squeakers.

Cecil said these girls lived just a little piece down the road from Mt. Pisgah Church. Well, since that church wasn't but about three miles from home, that didn't sound very far. He thought we should leave home about 1:00 in order to get there in plenty of time. I suggested that even though it wasn't very far we should maybe ride horses. He vetoed that idea since they didn't have any horse and he said he'd be darned if he'd go to see his girl riding any jackass. I even offered to let him ride my horse and I'd ride his mule. Nothing doing. We walked. It was just such a little piece down the road anyhow, he said.

We walked. And walked. A way on past that church. It was just a leetle bit further. I had long ago taken off my shoes and had the laces tied together and had them slung around my neck. Had my socks shoved down in em. He had his the same way. Next we took off our shirts and were trying to carry them so's they'd look reasonably fresh when we got there.

And HOT. Why, it was so hot that a lot of the fence posts had wilted. When we finally got within sight of their house, we put our clothes back on. Only I had lost a sock. And without that sock, in no time a tall those brand new, shiny, good smelling shoes had worn a whopping blister on my heel. So when we got there I was in extry good shape. I was hurting, hot, madder'n the mischief, and, since it was also right at suppertime, hungry.

Well sir, after eventually getting by two of the meanest looking bulldogs you ever saw and in on the front gallery—not a porch now, this was what everybody had down home, the front gallery—those two beautiful damsels joined us. So did their mama and papa, yeah, and so did three or four little brothers and sisters.

Wasn't long, though, until Mama had to go "fix a bite to eat." Then before you know it she hollered at Papa and the other youngans to come and eat. The girls told us they wouldn't be gone long. They weren't, and nobody asked us to eat even a crumb. They were real neighborly. Friendly and all.

Then it was time to go to church. We did get to walk beside our girls but in front of Mama and Papa and all the other youngans. Their church was only two miles from their house.

After church we walked em back home. I limped mine back. When we got back to their house their papa excused us at the front gate. I'm telling you the honest-to-goodness truth. He said he guessed we'd need to be getting on home since it was so late and all, and all country folks had to get up early.

What that old boy didn't know was that I had only one idea in my feeble mind and that was to get them new shoes off my feet. If that gal hadda been the Queen of Sheba, I wouldn't have been interested in going with her no place, not with those shoes on and as hungry as I was, and as mad.

I found out later that those two lovely young ladies lived 9 miles from us, so our round trip that afternoon and that night made a grand total of 22 miles—for a blind date.

But that was the ONLY time I ever got suckered into a deal like that. Though, you know what, old Cecil, my buddy, kept going back to see his girl and he kept fooling around until he wound up marrying her.

BLUE STAMPS FOR HUNG-OVER FOLKS

Did you ever begin a real important letter to somebody with one of those non-skid, no-skip, butter-writing fountain pens and have it go dry? Then have to use a pencil to finish your letter? That is the way our old cows used to do. They would go dry when we needed em most, and the only difference in this fountain pen business and a dry cow was it sure didn't help none to try to milk a pencil.

Talking about letter writing. With the price Uncle Sam has gone to charging for his stamps, it sure doesn't take long to use up a dollar's worth of them. I reckon inflation has hit the stamp business harder than nearly anything I can think of. Why I can remember when a 2¢ stamp would take a letter plumb to Arkansas, that is if you knew anybody that far off to mail a letter to. And a penny post card was good for near bout as far.

I know prices have gone up on nearly everything else too. For instance, I can remember when a loaf of bread sold for 10¢. And I could buy a dill pickle half as long as my arm for a nickel.

The bread you buy now is about 95¢. Course it is vitamin enriched. So, actually, you are getting a lot extra for your money. Well, you're not really getting anything more than we got back then. We just didn't know it and these bread people didn't know it either so we got em free. Then they found out about em being in there so now they charge us for telling us they are. I reckon it is worth something to know it.

But now you take stamps for a letter. The price has jumped 600% and post card stamps 900%. And to save my life I can't see how either of them has been improved one bit. Neither one will take your mail any farther than they used to, nor any faster either. Nor do we get our mail any oftener. Mine still comes just once a day and about the same time every morning. The glue on the back of the stamps still tastes just like it did years ago, so I am pretty hard put to figure out any new advantages or improvements in the stamp business.

I can think of several improvements which could be made in this racket, I mean business. The first one would be to offer stamps in 28 delicious flavors. I am pretty sure this would increase stamp sales no telling how much. People would probably write a lot more letters just to get to lick their favorite flavored stamps. Of course, I reckon I would stick with the old stand-bys: chocolate, vanilla, and strawberry. For the real exotic flavored stamp they could charge a little extra. Then, if they kept these old timey stamps like we have all been licking for a hundred years, they ought to cut the prices on them a right smart.

The shape of stamps is another thing that is getting mighty monotonous to me too. It seems to me like stamp designers could think of something besides rectangles, but apparently they are in a rut. Maybe if I mail a copy of this column to the Postmaster General it might help him out with this problem. I sure hope he can get the letter without my having to put his name on it. I have enough trouble trying to spell ordinary names like Smith, Brown, and Kelly.

In football season stamps ought to be shaped like a football, baseball season like a baseball. When the fish are biting, like a fish. You see, this idea has endless possibilities. Then, also, they should have some shaped and colored like the blossoms of different flowers. They would probably sell a lot of these to young folks who are courting. It might help the stamp business a lot if these flowered stamps were also scented. And with stamps being scented, flavored, and shaped, there is just no telling what this would do to the stamp business.

The only new thing the Post Office has come up with since I can remember is this ZIP CODE thing. Actually the only reason they came out with that was to sorta get in on this number fad which seems to be sweeping the country. This zip code idea doesn't seem to be ketching on too good though. And I predict they will soon give it up altogether on account of there are too many folks like me who can't hardly remember their own telephone numbers, let alone a flock of zip codes.

If they would put out some stamps shaped like arrow heads, this would help a lot I think. Then we could stick the stamp on the letter pointing in the direction it has to go. This would completely eliminate the need for zip codes which seem destined to go anyhow.

Another big help would be for the post office to have sales with bargains in stamps. Like six nickel stamps for a quarter. A pack of post cards for $6.25. Then they could have clearance sales in case any of their fancy flavored, peculiar shaped stamps were not selling too good.

On Mondays they oughta sell nothing but blue stamps. For folks with hangovers, they should sell stamps flavored with tomato juice and black coffee. To those who are looking forward to a big weekend, bourbon. If you prefer the local product, white lightning.

Then, finally, to give their stamp business a real shot in the arm, they oughta give green stamps with every purchase. These could be redeemed with postage stamps when we got our books full. This would help everybody's stamp business.

CUZ'S GLOSSARY

Cuz's columns reflected a unique writing style. They included a mixture of Smoky Mountain colloquialisms, south Alabama dialect, and phrases which Cuz himself coined. Following is a partial list which will aid the reader in his understanding of *Listening to the Grass Grow.''*

a gone to: planned to. "I's a gone to hoe the garden."
a holt of: hold of. "We'uns grabbed a holt of the mule."
ardine: iodine. "Maw put ardine on the cut."

bate: enough. "Junior et a bate of corn."
beller: yell. "Did you hear Claudus beller?"
bi-focuses: spectacles. "Paw can't read without his bifocuses."
BW: Beautiful Wife. "My BW cooked dinner for the preacher."

chillun: children. "How many chillun does he have?"
corker: unusual. "That feller shore was a corker!"

danged: almost. "He danged near fell asleep."

et: ate. "Christopher et two steaks."
extry: extra. "Maw gave me an extry big helping."

fit: fought. "The teams fit a hard game."
flipped my lid: mental breakdown. "All the pressure caused me to flip my lid."

gallery: front porch. "We stayed on the gallery so's we wouldn't get rained on."
get her dander up: anger. "She really got her dander up."

ketched: caught. "The dog ketched the rabbit."

kivvers: covers. "The room was so cold I had to pull the kivvers up."

lit a shuck: ran. "The boy was so skeered that he lit a shuck."

middling: medium. "I'll have a middling Coke."

monf: month. "There are twelve monfs in a year."

near bout: almost. "We are near bout home."

no sech: not such. "I never seed no sech a show."

overhauls: overalls. "He wore overhauls to hoe the corn."

passel: many, lots. "She cooked a passel o' turnips."

pecky: troublesome. "That toothache shore was pecky."

peel the bark: whip, spank. "His daddy really peeled the bark on him."

rough as a cob: difficult. "That test was rough as a cob."

shed of: rid of. "Did you get shed of the trash?"

slap: completely. "His car ran slap out of gas."

slue footed: walk unnaturally. "He drank so much he was slue footed."

snapped my wire: went berserk. "I's so mad I snapped my wire."

spanking new: brand new. "He had a spanking new car."

sto-boughten: purchased from a store. "Molly had a sto-boughten dress."

swarp: hit. "Did you see him swarp the dog?"

tetched: mentally unbalanced. "Sally was tetched so they sent her to the funny farm."

yo: ewe, female sheep. "He got a lot of wool from them twenty yos."

youngan: child. "How many youngans did he have?"

zapped: cut. "He zapped the watermelon."

zackly: exactly. "I gave him zackly enough."

RICK'S EPILOGUE

Daddy was no saint, but he did have several qualities that endeared him to many who knew him. Perhaps the best of these was his sense of humor. He liked to blend it with his efforts to help people with their sense of self esteem. One of his favorite expressions was "A warm pat on the back is better than flowers on a cold casket." This was boldly printed on the bottom of personal stationery he used with *The Cherokee Scout*.

Daddy's repertoire of folksy stories included one about an old mountaineer farmer who was discussing his mortality with a friend. His friend asked the farmer's preference for departing this life—whether he would prefer to die suddenly and unexpectedly, or whether he would rather become ill and linger along, and linger along, and linger along and die. The old farmer thought for awhile, spit out a mouthful of tobacco juice, scuffed his boots in the dirt, and began. "Well," he said, "I bleave I'd druther linger along, and linger along, and linger along and git well."

When Daddy became seriously ill, he lingered and lingered, but he didn't get well like the farmer wanted. However, he left the legacy of a collection of columns which his family and friends take pride in publishing. Somehow it seems that Daddy would realize a lot of satisfaction in seeing how things turned out.

—Rick Bagley
Cuz's Son

CHRISTOPHER'S EPILOGUE

I reckon one of Papa's favorite things to do was to make people feel real good about themselves. That and the fact that he LOVED to humor people. Once, I remember his telling me that a lady called and asked if this was Church's Fried Chicken. He replied, "No," but that he was "the chicken of the church." The lady laughed and pretty soon they had struck up a conversation. They talked for thirty minutes.

I suppose closest to the core of his heart were his kids and grandkids. He called me "MMM" (My Main Man). One of the things he loved to do with me was challenge my mind. I loved the topic of Presidents, and he would enjoy spending as much as an hour at a time quizzing me on the subject. When I was five, I had the ambition to "grow up and be the best President in the world." Of course, being only a little tyke, and not even able to make up my own bed, I had no idea how I would handle such a big job. But Papa believed I could do anything I set my mind to.

Much of what I remember about Papa was his hilarious and realistic stories. Reading them again seems to bring back a whole part of my life.

—Christopher Bagley
Cuz's Grandson